And We
Sold
the Rain

Contemporary Fiction
from Central America

Edited by Rosario Santos

Four Walls Eight Windows
New York

First printing Oct., 1988.

Library of Congress Cataloging-in-Publication Data
And we sold the rain : contemporary fiction from Central America /
    edited by Rosario Santos.
        p. cm.
    ISBN 0-941423-16-6 : $18.95. ISBN 0-941423-17-4 (pbk.) : $9.95
        1. Central American fiction—20th century—Translations into
English.   2. English fiction—Translations from Spanish.   3. Short
stories, Central American—Translations into English.   4. Short
stories, English—Translations from Spanish.   I. Santos, Rosario.
PQ7477.E5A54   1988
863'.01'089728—dc19   88-21299
                                                                    CIP

Four Walls Eight Windows
P.O. Box 548
Village Station
New York, N.Y. 10014

Designed by Martin Moskof.
Printed in the U.S.A.
First edition.

Contents

Preface   vii
Rosario Santos

Introduction   ix
Jo Anne Engelbert

Look at Lislique, See How Pretty It Is   1
Jacinta Escudos (*El Salvador*)

The Proof   7
Rodrigo Rey Rosa (*Guatemala*)

Anita the Insect Catcher   13
Roberto Castillo (*Honduras*)

Confinement   27
Horacio Castellanos Moya (*Honduras*)

Story of the Maestro Who Spent His Whole
Life Composing a Piece for the Marimba   35
Mario Payeras (*Guatemala*)

Guatemala 1954—Funeral for a Bird   43
Arturo Arias (*Guatemala*)

I Am René Espronceda de la Barca   51
Leonel Rugama (*Nicaragua*)

For These Things My Name Is René   61
Mario Roberto Morales (*Guatemala*)

April in the Forenoon   75
Julio Escoto (*Honduras*)

The Perfect Game   89
Sergio Ramírez (*Nicaragua*)

In the Shade of a Little Old Lady in Flower   107
Alfonso Quijada Urías (*El Salvador*)

Tarantulas of Honey   115
Pedro Rivera (*Panama*)

A March Guayacan   125
Bertalicia Peralta (*Panama*)

Microbus to San Salvador   131
Manlio Argueta (*El Salvador*)

Sodom   143
Samuel Rovinski (*Costa Rica*)

And We Sold the Rain   149
Carmen Naranjo (*Costa Rica*)

The Dog   157
Lyzandro Chávez Alfaro (*Nicaragua*)

Boardinghouse   171
Claribel Alegría (*El Salvador*)

Mr. Taylor   183
Augusto Monterroso (*Guatemala*)

Self-Defense   191
Fabián Dobles (*Costa Rica*)

Authors' Biographies   201

Translators' Biographies   211

Acknowledgments   213

Preface

Ever since Central America became a daily item in the news, I have been concerned by the way its people, their history and their culture, are ignored, their lives reduced to abstract concepts and code words, like "banana republic," "guerrilla war," and "contra aid," their voices suffocated.

Such was my motivation for compiling this collection. In search of these voices, I turned to the literature produced by Central American writers, looking for the stories that would convey the magic, the myths, the beliefs and the culture that nurture and maintain the Central American spirit.

I came across dozens of writers whose work provided rich and abundant material from which to choose. My first impulse for a historical survey was later supplanted by the need to stay close to the present reality and to hear the voices of contemporary writers. Thus, the final selection is dominated by Central American writing of the last decade and the result, I think, is impressive. With few exceptions, these writers are unknown in the United States. They have been writing and publishing their work in the most precarious of circumstances in times of war and struggle. Most importantly, they are witnesses to their time and are recording their history. What they write must make us think and wonder.

My hope is that these stories, in their diversity, will begin to open the mind of the reader to an essential understanding of Central America and its people and will serve to counterbalance the dehumanizing effect of media reporting.

While working on the selection, several people were extremely helpful and gave me much needed encouragement and support. I am especially grateful to Jo Anne Engelbert, Roberto Sosa and Carmen Naranjo for their continuous support. I also wish to express special thanks to the authors for authorizing me to publish their stories; to the translators for their enthusiasm and cooperation; to Zoe Anglesey for lending me very useful material; and to the editors at Four Walls Eight Windows, Dan Simon and John Oakes, who shared my concern and enthusiasm for the project, and made this book possible.

My gratitude as well to the New York Foundation for the Arts/New York State Council on the Arts, for the translation grant which was essential to the completion of this volume.

—Rosario Santos
New York, NY
Sept, 1988

Introduction

*Living is going to Xibalba
and playing the ballgame worthily.*

—Julio Fausto Aguilera

Eyes aglow, the Spaniards clutched the sides of the basket that was to take them down, the Indians assured them, to the ultimate golden trove. Patiently, and with infinite satisfaction, the Indians played out the ropes until at last the heat of the volcano reached the kindling temperature of reeds and hemp, and the Spaniards fell freely toward their hearts' desire.

This fantastic tale was told and retold in Central America until at last it became history by virtue of the truth it incarnated—a necessary story, invented with wit and will as a means of insuring survival.

Throughout Central American history, stories have opened an imaginative channel for commentary and dissent. Alongside pious myths, colonial homilies and cloying patriarchal tales, imagination has kept hope and dignity alive in the form of stories recorded at the margin of official discourse. In this vast legacy of stories, the rabbit frequently confounds the jackal, the humble vanquish the arrogant. The theme is an ancient one in the fragile isthmus where conquest and subjugation were familiar realities long before the arrival of Europeans.

The sacred book of the Mayas, the *Popol Vuh*, contains among its magical tales of sorcery and revelation the cycle of feats of twin heroes, Ixbalanqué and Hunhunapú. With cunning and valor the two young ballplayers defeat the dark Lords of Xibalba, a tenebrous underworld that included even then a house of fear, a house of knives. Each generation has adapted the heroes' story to its own needs; in the course of Central American history the dark lords have assumed many forms.

Fiction's infinite potential for subversion was not lost upon the Inquisition, which forbade in the Spanish colonies the reading and writing of works of the imagination. Romances, books of chivalry and other form of "deceitful narration" were officially banned, ostensibly to protect the newly catechized Indians against superstition. Fiction was suspect; the fewer tales of dragon slayers in circulation, the better. The conquest over, the colonies needed to nurture not heroes but functionaries. With respect to written texts, the ban on fiction was effective. The development of both the novel and the short story was delayed in Spanish America until the nineteenth century. But the human need to hear and tell stories lies beyond the reach of bulls and edicts. Even as the Inquisitorial flames licked up such seditious fare as *Don Quixote de la Mancha*, the story went underground and surfaced in unexpected times, places and ways, but most importantly in the oral tradition.

> FRIAR FRANCISCO DE BOBADILLA: "How did you learn what you have just told me?"
> CHIEF MISESBOY: "Our fathers told us this, and we hold it to be true."
> FRIAR: "Do you have books like this one" (he shows him a Bible) "where such things are recorded?"
> CHIEF: "No."

FRIAR: "Since you have no books, how did you remember all you have just told me?"
CHIEF: "Our ancestors told us these things and
passed them down to us in the form of stories."
FRIAR: "Have you told these things to your children?"
CHIEF: "Yes, and I have told them that they must
hold them in their memory so they can tell them
to their children . . . so that knowledge of them
will not be lost. This is how I and the other Indians now alive learned these things."[1]

Among the indigenous peoples of Central America,
story telling was a sacred art cultivated with care and
refinement. Highly esteemed members of the community, storytellers received elaborate training, commit-
ting to memory the entire secular and religious history
of their people—hundreds of narratives—which they
kept alive through constant retelling. The conquest
violently interrupted this ancient tradition, and most of
the legends, myths and fables were lost as the Indians
were converted to Christianity. What survived of the
tradition was the Indians' delight in telling stories and
their skill in using fable and allegory as means of
conveying a painful or dangerous message.

The Spaniards brought with them a tradition of story
telling that had its origins in the Middle Ages and that
thrived as well in the plazas and inns of Central America as it had in Spain. In time the blend of Indian and
Spanish traditions gave rise to a new genre of folktale
called *cuentos de camino* or "stories of the road." The
genre has survived into the twentieth century and
continues to be, according to novelist Sergio Ramírez,
the richest vein of Central American narrative.[2]

Many "stories of the road" are horror stories, echoes
of the trauma and devastation of the conquest. The

legends of the *carreta nagua* or phantom death cart, an oxcart that rolls through deserted streets at night with a hellish din, carrying dead bodies or skeletons, has a basis in the bloody business of colonial repression. Caravans of oxcarts were used by Spanish soldiers who raided villages at night in search of slaves. "Behind the phantasmagoria there lies an ancient fear, a history of ancestral terror," according to Nicaraguan folklorist Milagros Palma. "Our people, like many another, has recorded its history in its collective memory and eternalized it through a system of encoding."[3]

In Guatemala, where two thirds of the Indians perished between 1519 and 1610, the conquest left wounds that would not heal. An Indian poet wrote of the *dzules* or strangers,

> *They taught fear.*
> *They came to wither the flowers.*
> *So that their flower might live*
> *they crushed and sucked the nectar out of ours.*
>
> *To castrate the sun!*
> *That is what the dzules came to do.*
> *The sons of their sons remain,*
> *here in the midst of the people.*
> *We taste the bitter gall.*[4]

Out of the fear and outrage, storytellers developed forms of encoding or masking their allusions to individuals and events. A familiar story line, such as the pact with the devil, might be adapted to register anger against a local plantation owner who was mistreating his workers. The storyteller, without even mentioning the *patrón* by name, could suggest that he had become wealthy by selling his immortal soul. In many stories the arrogant rich were depicted after death as pitiable wraiths who accosted travelers in the moonlight to press coins into their hands; the ironic punishment for their greed was to wander the earth giving away money until all their wealth was equitably distributed. Some storytellers used only animals as characters, easily identifiable as villains or heroes. La Llorona, the tragic weeping woman of Mexican and Central American folklore, is a blend of Indian and Spanish elements.

The basic tale, repeated throughout the Americas, portrays the abuse of native women by European men. La Llorona is a beautiful young woman who is seduced by a white man by whom she has three children. Brutally spurned by him, La Llorona goes mad and in some versions of the story kills the babies she cannot care for. Her fate is to roam dark streets for all eternity weeping for her children. Some sources identify her with the Aztec goddess Matlacíuatl, "a vampire-like creature who stalks desolate places feeding on men." Other folklorists believe she is Ciuapipiltín, a goddess who ventures forth at midnight carrying an empty cradle, looking for her lost children.[5] While in her origins La Llorona constituted a bitter protest against the exploitation of Indian women by the conquistadors, her figure has come to symbolize all victims of machismo. Clearly, the "story of the road" became a genre in which popular imagination could express sorrow, pain, and rage, reflect on contemporary events, and register dissent.

Colonial authorities did everything in their power to efface all vestiges of the indigenous past. When the Aztec and Mayan capitals were razed, thousands of pages of historical pictographs were burned, including entire libraries of painted books. While priests transcribed some sacred texts like the *Popol Vuh*, these were not permitted to circulate until the nineteenth century. Occasionally this amputation of history, coupled with a rigid censorship, was successful in "colonizing the imagination," as critic Jean Franco puts it. On the slopes of the volcano Mombacho in Nicaragua, campesinos tell the following story of creation:

> The devil wanted to put his people in the world and the Lord Jesus did also, but the Lord won out because he was more powerful, and all the Indians, who were the people the devil had created, went away. . . . Those Indians became monkeys and went off to live in the jungle. They have arrows to kill the civilized people, whom they fear.[6]

In another version of the same story, the Indians were the first people God created. But they killed Jesus Christ, so God punished them by changing them into monkeys.

As Milagros Palma points out, such stories bear testimony to the tragedy of a people cut off from a knowledge of their own past and taught to feel such revulsion for their history that they can no longer recognize themselves in it. Against the powerful ideologies imposing themselves in the isthmus, the ancient strategies of the embattled storyteller—parable and allegory, parody and satire, fable and fantastic tale—were in colonial times, as now, invaluable arms in the struggle to ransom the abducted past, to delineate and to denounce a repressive present.

Emancipation brought the first attempts toward the recovery of the truncated past and the definition of national identity. But the self-appointed definers of that identity were for the most part plantation owners or their peers, members of an elite who amused their friends by writing picturesque stories of rural life, exalting nature and a Divine Providence that had distributed land and wealth with such unerring wisdom.

These tales depicted a patriarchal paradise where campesinos, in their sandals and palm frond hats, are always the salt of the earth, amiable chuckleheads who are happy (of course) but pitiably lacking in education (witness their amusing speech) and sensitivity (look how they live!). Manuals of literature honor these stories as the origins of the national literatures of Central America. In truth, these works actually retarded the development of national literatures.

But at the margin of this treacly celebration of the status quo, the popular imagination continued its authentic labor of invention:

> A butcher went to the ranch of a wealthy cattleman and bought a beautiful cow to slaughter. That night no one could sleep because that cow began to cry out in a sorrowful voice, not mooing but moaning or sobbing. . . . At midnight everyone went to the butcher's house, for he was about to kill the cow. The cow's moans were terrible. When the butcher raised the knife, tears began to fall from her big sad eyes. The butcher put the knife away; everybody knew the cow was a human being. They knew that when people disappear, they are often changed into animals. . . . It's happened to lots of people around here; they've become the cattle of the rich. . . .[7]

It would be a long time before the comical, lyrical, macabre material of the popular tale could energize literary narrative in Central America. So long as few could read, story telling flourished primarily as a folk art. Toward the end of the nineteenth century, however, literacy increased and the growth of cities brought newspapers whose literary pages provided the long-awaited space in which the short story could finally develop as an art form and as a medium of national expression.

A critical element in the evolution of the short story in Central America was the invention of a language, a new Spanish, expanded and refined, cleansed of euphemisms and clichés and capable of giving expression to a bewildering and contradictory reality. To a great extent this language was the bequest of a single poet, the Nicaraguan Rubén Darío. Darío not only renovated Spanish but ended the isolation that had caused Hispanic literature to stagnate. He also served as the conduit through which Baudelaire and Mallarmé, Valéry and Lautreamont, Poe, Whitman and many other writers cross-pollinated Hispanic letters, giving rise to a brilliant period of creativity called Modernism that produced not only poets but short story writers.

Darío arrived at a time when "the Colossus of the North" had begun to intervene ever more flagrantly in the internal affairs of Latin American states. A significant aspect of his legacy is his political forthrightness, as may be seen in his 1905 poem "To Roosevelt."

> *United States, you are powerful and great.*
> *When you quake, a deep tremor*
> *passes along the enormous vertebrae of the*
>   *Andes.*
> *If you shout, your voice is heard as the roar of*
>   *a lion.*
>   . . .
>
> *But our America which had poets*
> *from the ancient days of Netzahualcoyotl,*
> *which has conserved the footprints of the great*
>   *Bacchus;*
> *which once learned the panic alphabet;*
> *which consulted the stars and knew Atlantis,*

whose name comes echoing to us all the way
from Plato,
which from the earliest moments of its life
lives on light, on fire, on perfume and on love;
the America of the great Montezuma, of the
Inca,
the fragrant America of Christopher Colum-
bus,
Catholic America, Spanish America,
the America in which the noble Cuauhtémoc
said:
"I am not in a bed of roses"; that America
that trembles with hurricanes and lives on love,
oh men with Saxon eyes, lives.
And dreams. And trembles with love, and is
the daughter of the Sun.
Beware. Spanish America is alive!
A thousand cubs now whelped by the Spanish
lion are now free.

Darío's influence was a powerful one throughout the Hispanic world, but nowhere more so than in Central America, where both his standards of excellence and his political clarity challenged poets, novelists and short story writers to continue his initiatives. Most of Central America's greatest writers owe something to Darío, if only the realization that Central America need not remain in the backwaters of literature. When Guatemalan novelist Miguel Angel Asturias won the Nobel Prize for such novels as *El Señor Presidente, Men of Maize, The Eyes of the Interred, Mulata* and an extraordinary trilogy denouncing the United Fruit Company, all the world knew that Central American literature had come of age. Asturias combined material from the oral tradition, the *Popol Vuh* and current history in complex, often surreal narratives that introduced into Central American fiction what the rest of the world was learning from William Faulkner, John Dos Passos and James Joyce. The period documented by Asturias brought a new humiliation, the banana republic. Pablo Neruda called it "the tyrannical Reign of the Flies":

> *Trujillo the fly, and Tacho the fly,*
> *the flies called Carías, Martínez,*
> *Ubico—all of them flies, flies*
> *dank with the blood of their marmalade*
> *vassalage, flies buzzing drunkenly*
> *on the populous middens . . .* [8]

The "flies," puppet dictators maintained in power by the United States to advance corporate interests in the region, fattened on filth. Neruda mentions only a few of them: Rafael Leonidas Trujillo of the Dominican Republic (1931–1960); Anastasio (Tacho) Somoza of Nicaragua (1936–1956) succeeded by two of his sons, Luis (1956–1967) and Anastasio (1967–1979); Tiburcio Carías of Honduras (1933–1948); Maximiliano Hernández Martínez of El Salvador (1931–1944) and Jorge Ubico of Guatemala (1931–1944). There were others as well, and all had much in common.

While selling out the resources of their countries to United States investors in return for political and military support, the dictators allowed their people to be cruelly exploited and cooperated in bloody actions to break strikes, terrorize union organizers and prevent the rise of political opposition. Most found it necessary to use increasingly repressive measures in order to remain in power. On January 22, 1932, when impoverished Salvadoran peasants armed with stones and machetes attacked landowners' mansions, Martínez' military forces conducted a systematic massacre called La Matanza in which 30,000 Salvadorans, more than two percent of the population, were killed in one week. Anyone wearing the traditional clothing of the Indians could be picked out and shot, and peasants became so fearful that they stopped using their native languages and typical dress. Martínez ruled for twelve more years after La Matanza.[9] Guatemala became a police state under Ubico, who made it a crime for an Indian not to work on one of the foreign-owned plantations, for starvation wages. With excessive concessions, corporations made unprecedented profits on which they paid no taxes—they just paid off the dictator, who was usually able to amass a huge personal fortune. When the first Somoza was assassinated by a poet in 1956, his assets totaled $60,000,000. His second son was far more successful. When the Sandinista forces took power in 1979, Anastasio Somoza Debayle was one of the wealthiest men in the world, and the Somoza family controlled nearly one fourth of Nicaraguan territory.[10]

The United States attitude toward the dictators was cynical and self-serving. Franklin Roosevelt summed it up perfectly in his often-quoted remark, "Somoza is a son-of-a-bitch, but he's our son-of-a-bitch."

Madness and pathological cruelty seem to have been requisites for office. The first Somoza had a penchant for the dramatic and kept a collection of costumes and props. He staged various massacres for which he dressed up his soldiers like Roman legionnaires. Jorge Ubico considered himself another Napoleon and surrounded himself with busts and portraits of the Emperor who, he said, had the same profile. Of Salvadoran dictator Hernández Martínez, it was said "He believed in military discipline: he militarized the post office employees, school children and the symphony orchestra. . . . Maximiliano Hernández Martínez, a vegetarian and theosophist, believed he was protected by 'invisible legions' who were in direct telepathic communication with the President of the United States."[11] David Kirsh also recorded about Hernández Martínez, "When the local archbishop begged him in the name of God to spare the lives of arrested opponents, he replied, 'In El Salvador, I am God.'"[12]

No country of Central America escaped the scourge of dollar diplomacy. For the banana republics, Guatemala, Nicaragua, Honduras, and El Salvador, the consequences of "the reign of the flies" were decades of fear and deprivation and an abominable legacy of hunger, illiteracy and disease.

But not even Neruda could have foreseen the chaos and horror of recent events in Central America, nor the enormous difficulty of reporting these events to the world. As never before, writers must be what Carlos Fuentes has called "the voice of those who have no voice." He writes:

> In countries subjected to the pendular oscillation between dictatorship and anarchy, in which the only constant is exploitation, countries bereft of democratic channels of expression, without systems of public information, responsible parliaments, independent trade unions or an emanicipated intellectual class, the writer must be, simultaneously, legislator and reporter, revolutionary and thinker.[13]

The writer must also be exceptionally courageous, for in many Central American countries writers have been among the prime targets of repressive regimes. The list of writers who have lost their lives as a consequence of political dissidence is very long. It includes Guatemalans Otto René Castillo, Roberto Obregón, López Valdizón and Oscar Palencia; Salvadorans José

María Cuéllar, Roque Dalton, Rigoberto Góngora and Jaime Suárez; Nicaraguans Rigoberto López Pérez (executed for assassinating the first Somoza), Roberto Morales Avilés, Edwin Castro, Pedro Joaquín Chamorro and an author represented in this book, Leonel Rugama. There are many others.

Literature has played a significant role in liberation movements in Central America, particularly in Nicaragua, whose Vice President is distinguished novelist and short-story writer Sergio Ramírez and whose minister of culture is one of Latin America's leading poets, Ernesto Cardenal. Leonel Rugama, whose story "I Am René Espronceda de la Barca," is included here, was killed in the insurrection at the age of twenty. His ironic narrative ridicules the posturings of the kind of intellectual who saves his skin by taking the high ground whenever possible, the polar opposite of Central America's best writers.

Many Guatemalans know by heart the writings of poets whose works are not for sale in bookstores. Otto René Castillo, who was captured by the military in 1967, tortured, and burned alive when he refused to reveal the names of members of the resistance movement, is one of the few idols of the young, as is Roberto Obregón, who disappeared in 1970 on the border between Guatemala and El Salvador. Obregón used as the epigram for his poem "The Inscriptions" a phrase from the *Popol Vuh*: "*Lo que quieren es acabar con nosotros*—Their intention is to kill us all." The work of Salvadoran writers in exile—Manlio Argueta in Costa Rica, Claribel Alegría in Nicaragua, Roberto Armijo in France, Alfonso Quijada Urías in Canada, to mention just a few—circulates within their countries and has served to create throughout the world an awareness of the plight of the Salvadoran peasant. Several Honduran writers have been outspoken critics of their government's servile compliance with foreign interests. Poet Roberto Sosa writes about the poor—"the weariness of the peasants who cut the grass outweighs the universe"—and of the machinations of the generals "who buy, interpret and distribute words and silence." His book *Military Secret* is a gallery of portraits of Latin American strongmen. Costa Rican and Panamanian writers denounce economic oppression and the psychological and cultural consequences of dependency; the stories included here by Carmen Naranjo and Pedro Rivera are excellent examples of this effort. What little is known outside the region about Central America has been largely divulged through fiction and poetry.

The stories in this collection are among the first from Central America to appear in English. They are meant to serve as a counterpoise to the sensationalism of media reporting that demeans and dehumanizes the tragedy of recent history. They remind us that behind the contorted masks of tabloid photography exist men and women who work and make love, buy bread and wash their children's faces. For example, some of these stories provide a fleeting sense of what it may feel like to live in Honduras or Costa Rica by allowing us to listen to the quiet voices of people engaged in daily life. Rooted in the nervous tradition of Central American story telling, they reflect a long experience of writing in a climate of restraint and fear. In this latitude every writer must create a system of allusions for speaking the unspeakable, for political realities are always perilously near.

Not surprisingly, the focus of much of Central American fiction is the green hell of guerrilla warfare. Jacinta Escudos uses the voice of a very young fighter from a tiny village, Lislique, to epitomize El Salvador's ongoing tragedy: "I would have told you, Jaime, 'Look at Lislique, how pretty it is without the *guardia*.'" In Roberto Morales's story, "For These Things My Name Is René," the pervasiveness of the ideal of the guerrilla is manifested in its ability to haunt the consciences of those who feel they have fallen short. And to witness, in Chávez Alfaro's "The Dog," the furious revulsion felt by the dog's mistress for the animal's defection to the camp of William Walker is to have an inkling of the massive ire inspired in Central America by Walker, his filibusters and their twentieth-century counterparts. While Arturo Arias, in "Guatemala 1954—Funeral for a Bird," portrays the horror of the days immediately following the U.S.-instigated coup that overthrew the government of Jacobo Arbenz, through the eyes of a four-and-a-half-year-old child playing in city streets littered with rotting corpses.

If Central America's trauma has caused unprecedented suffering, it has also tempered values, clarified motives, and given rise to a heightened reverence for life. If many story writers are performing an exorcism of horror, others are creating a new logos of hope and strength, as in Mario Payeras's "Story of the Maestro Who Spent His Whole Life Composing a Piece for the Marimba," a parable of reconciliation, or Sergio Ramírez's "The Perfect Game," so attentive to the details of the commonplace as it celebrates the ethic of earnestness at a Nicaraguan baseball game that we claim it as an analogue for something larger.

To read these stories is to rediscover the vitality of fiction. In Central America the story is performing its primordial function of mediating history, interpreting a brutal and brutalizing reality, and keeping hope and dignity alive, as it has for centuries on this frail bridge between worlds.

—Jo Anne Engelbert
Montclair, NJ
July 1988

NOTES

1. Milagros Palma, *Por los senderos míticos de Nicaragua*, (Managua: Editorial Nueva Nicaragua, 1984), p. 13. Fragment of an interview in the Plaza Teoca de Xalteva, in Granada, Nicaragua, September 28, 1538.

2. *Antología del cuento centroamericano*, Prologue, selection and notes by Sergio Ramírez, (San Jose: EDUCA, 1984), p. 17.

3. Palma, pp. 159-60.

4. Miguel León Portilla, *El reverso de la conquista*, (Mexico: Editorial Joaquín Mortiz, 1964), p. 78. Fragment of a Mayan text, the *Chilam Balam of Chumayel*.

5. Antonia Castañeda Shular, Tomás Ybarra-Frausto, Joseph Sommers, *Literatura chicana*, (Englewood Cliffs, New Jersey: Prentice-Hall, 1972), p. 97.

6. Palma, p. 184.

7. Ibid, p. 123.

8. Pablo Neruda, "The United Fruit Company," in *Selected Poems of Pablo Neruda*, edited and translated by Ben Belitt, (New York: Grove Press, 1961), p. 149.

9. David Kirsh, *Central America Without Crying Uncle*, (New York: Primer Project, 1987), p. 9.

10. *Ibid*, p. 44.

11. Eduardo Galeano, *Open Veins of Latin America*, quoted in *Dollars and Dictators*, by Tom Barry, Beth Wood and Deb Preusch, (New York: Grove Press, 1983), p. 5.

12. Kirsh, p. 9.

13. Carlos Fuentes, *La nueva novela hispanoamericana*, (Mexico: Editorial Joaquín Mortiz, 1969), p. 12.

Look at Lislique, See How Pretty It Is

Jacinta Escudos

Ah, to return to Lislique, return to its trees, its fresh and quiet afternoons. Lislique. But the Lislique I knew as a kid— with its cobblestone streets, its white houses full of ancient secrets, and the *niña* María on the corner telling her apes to come back home, not to go too far, and those pains in the ass sneaking into neighbors' farms and stealing oranges and guayabas. Then would come the complaints, the fights with the woman next door, and you're in deep shit with the mayor . . .

Lislique, where Jaime once dreamed of joining the Eagles, "eight times national champs and one time almost champions of the Central American Cup." He said he was as good as Cariota Barraza, and he was, or even better, although he wasn't a lefty, but he was the best halfback on the Cornelio Reyna Soccer Club. He wanted to go to the capital, to play on the Flor Blanca Club, but he'd never been any farther than La Unión, which he liked a lot, swearing that maybe that's what San Salvador was like. If he had gone there, for sure he would've gotten scared by so many buildings, streets, people, cars.

Lislique and the mango tree nearby on the road where Jaime and I used to tease the girls that went by, or where we'd sit and shoot the bull, or take cover when the *guardia* came looking for anyone they might grab and draft by force. But sometimes we hung around, you know, for love . . . Jaime would stop by to see Colombia every night, and I would stand lookout, and just when they were in the heat of things, someone would run by warning "the *guardia!* the *guardia!*" and we'd high tail it out of there.

We listened to *rancheras* on the radio, and when Cornelio won a game, Jaime would get all excited and go on and on about joining the Eagles. The poor guy was such an incurable soccer fan I could only laugh. But sometimes he would get sad and stare at a tree up ahead; maybe he was still thinking of Colombia.

He'd stay glued to the radio in case she'd sent him a message or dedicated a song by the Tigres del Norte on the station from Chaparrastique. In those days he was already a goner—the *guardia* really had it in for him.

Maybe we'll be able to return to Lislique forever when this goddamn fucking shitass war is over. There aren't enough insults in the world to curse it good and proper just like there won't be joy enough to celebrate when we win.

I left Lislique, left everything behind—the family, the townspeople and Jaime—and got to know other people, other places, but I couldn't get it out of my head that there was no other town like Lislique. Now I think I understand what Juan from Jocoro used to say when he visited the family. He'd say that your real country is your childhood, which is to say Lislique in my case. I was sure that in Lislique you could make a go of things. Jaime and I had already decided to open a carpentry shop. We'd stay in Lislique until we died; we'd have a home, a wife, children. Jaime sometimes even forgot about joining the Eagles, so much did he just want to be a Lisliqueño, and so much did he like the idea of having a trade and a house of his own.

Damn, and here I am returning. I never imagined I'd come back this way, still having to hide at two in the afternoon, making my way amid the pasture grounds, not being able to sit down in the Negrita Express Bar to listen to *La Carta Número Tres* and chat with Lucio who surely still drives a truck. What a homecoming, with a pile of memories that get confused with my heartbeats, my trigger finger all numb from keeping it arched, my knapsack weighing me down.

We returned to Lislique. They made me come too because most of the *compas* didn't know the place, so I had to help draw the map and scout the terrain way ahead of the battalion. Here we were invading Lislique, and it felt so good to see the little town and all the townspeople who came out to see us after we kicked the shit out of the *guardia*. Damn, we were all moved to find old friends, family, and *niña* María saying man how good you look in that guerrilla get-up, and Lucio that I'm a real wiseguy, and all of us a bunch of rascals, and my mom shouting that I shouldn't go on but happy anyway to see me and find me well. Wow, what a gathering! Everyone was there, if you only knew how pretty it is to see such a gathering in your own town that you've just taken and everyone you know is there . . . well, almost everyone.

Jaime wasn't there. He wasn't there to see Lislique liberated, the great liberation. "See how pretty the town looks without the *guardia*," I would've said to him, and we would've gone to shoot the bull by the mango tree which must have gotten bigger by now.

But Lislique, damn . . . life is a real bitch at times, Jaime. What did I know, buddy; how could I have known? No one, damn it, no one thought of sending me the news: Jaime's a soldier because he didn't get his shit together and split, so the *guardia* got him and drafted him by force. So there was Jaime with La Unión Company, going to take back control, or so they thought, of Cerro Zopilote, which was in our hands. Jaime the soldier, without Lislique, you fell dead in the ambush. Jaime, your ass grassed by the *guardia* and forced to become a soldier, without the mango tree, without Colombia, without the Eagles, without your radio. Jaime, you stayed in town with your bullheaded desire to be a soccer star. You didn't want to come with us; you even cursed me and told me that you couldn't give a shit about the soldiers, the *compas* or the war. You stayed, thinking nothing was going to happen to you, but you got fucked, you did. The *guardia* came by; they forced you to join, and I didn't know it, and now I find myself approaching a corpse, and I see and don't believe it's you, Jaime buddy. I bend over and smooth the hair that got all tousled on your forehead and that Colombia once kissed and now it's all full of the blood, sweat, earth, dust, time, and sadness of this war without Lislique. And me in this gathering, and all the townspeople shouting slogans, and Lislique forever-more without you.

I think about you dead over there. I couldn't bury you. We had to leave; others stayed, but I had to come to the town, so you stayed there all alone. On my way I kept thinking that at five o'clock the buzzards would come if you and the others weren't buried soon, and for sure it wouldn't be soon enough, and then the buzzards would—

Look at Lislique, Jaime. Look at Lislique now without the *guardia* shaking people down. Look at Lislique all full of *compas*, the little red flag waving down there on the plaza where you met Colombia—look how pretty it all is . . .

Translated by George Yúdice

The Proof

Rodrigo Rey Rosa

One night while his parents were still on the highway returning from someone's birthday party, Miguel went into the living room and stopped in front of the canary's cage. He lifted up the cloth covering the cage and opened the tiny door. Fearfully, he slipped his hand inside, and then withdrew it doubled into a fist, with the bird's head protruding between his fingers. It allowed itself to be seized almost without resistance, showing the resignation of a person with a chronic illness, thinking perhaps that it was being taken out so the cage could be cleaned and the seeds replenished. But Miguel was staring at it with the eager eyes of one seeking an omen.

All the lights in the house were turned on. Miguel had gone through all the rooms, hesitating at each corner. God can see you no matter where you are, Miguel told himself, but there are not many places suitable for invoking Him. Finally he decided on the cellar because it was dark there. In a corner under the high vaulted ceiling, he crouched as Indians and savages do, face down, his arms wrapped around his legs, holding the canary in his fist between his knees. Raising his eyes into the darkness, which at that moment looked red, he said in a low voice: "If you exist, God, bring this bird back to life." As he spoke, he tightened his fist little by little, until his fingers felt the snapping of the fragile bones and an unaccustomed stillness in the little body.

Then, without meaning to, he remembered María Luisa the maid, who took care of the canary. A little later, when he finally opened his hand, it was as if another, larger hand had been placed on his back—the hand of fear. He realized that the bird would not come back to life. If God did not exist, it was absurd to fear His punishment. The image, the concept of God went out of his mind, leaving a blank. Then, for an instant, Miguel thought of the shape of evil, of Satan, but he did not dare ask anything of him.

He heard the sound of the car going into the garage over his head. Now the fear had to do with this world. His parents had arrived; he heard their voices, heard the car doors slam and the sound of a woman's heels on the stone floor. He laid the inert little body on the floor in the corner, groped in the dark for a loose brick, and set it on top of the bird. Then he heard the chiming of the bell at the front door, and ran upstairs to greet his parents.

"All the lights on!" exclaimed his mother as he kissed her.

"What were you doing down there?" his father asked him.

"Nothing. I was afraid. The empty house scares me."

His mother went through the house, turning lights off right and left, secretly astonished by her son's fear.

That night Miguel had his first experience of insomnia. For him not sleeping was a kind of nightmare from which there was no hope of awakening. A static nightmare: the dead bird beneath the brick, and the empty cage.

Hours later Miguel heard the front door open, and the sound of footsteps downstairs. Paralyzed by fear, he fell asleep. María Luisa the maid had finally arrived. It was seven o'clock; the day was still dark. She turned on the kitchen light, set her basket on the table, and, as was her custom, removed her sandals in order not to make any noise. She went into the living room and uncovered the canary's cage. The little door was open and the cage was empty. After a moment of panic, during which her eyes remained fixed on the cage hanging in front of her, she glanced around, covered the cage again and returned to the kitchen. Very carefully she took up her sandals and the basket, and went out. When she was no longer in sight of the house she put the sandals on and started to run in the direction of the market, where she hoped to find another canary. It was necessary to replace the one which she thought had escaped due to her carelessness.

Miguel's father awoke at quarter past seven. He went down to the kitchen and, surprised to see that María Luisa had not yet come, decided to go to the cellar for the oranges and squeeze them himself. Before going back up to the kitchen, he tried to turn off the light, but with his hands and arms laden with oranges, he had to use his shoulders to push the switch. One of the oranges slipped from his arm and rolled across the floor into a corner. He pushed the light on once more. Placing the oranges on a chair, he formed a bag out of the front of his bathrobe, dropped the oranges into it, and went to pick up the one in the corner. And then he noticed the bird's wing sticking out from under the brick. It was not easy for him, but he could guess what had happened. Everyone knows that children are cruel, but how should he react? His wife's footsteps sounded above him in the kitchen. He was ashamed of his son, and at the same time he felt that they were accomplices. He had to hide the shame and the guilt as if they were his own. He picked up the brick, put the bird in his bathrobe pocket, and climbed up to the kitchen. Soon he went on upstairs to his room to wash and dress.

A little later, as he left the house, he met María Luisa returning from the market with the new canary hidden in her basket. She greeted him in an odd fashion, but he did not notice it. He was upset: the hand that he kept in his pocket held the bird in it.

As María Luisa went into the house, she heard the voice of Miguel's mother on the floor above. She put the basket on the floor, took out the canary, and ran to slip it into the cage, which she then uncovered with an air of relief and triumph. However, when she drew back the window curtains and the sun's rays tinted the room pink, she saw with alarm that the bird had one black foot.

It was impossible to awaken Miguel. His mother had to carry him into the bathroom, where she turned on the tap and with her wet hand gave his face a few slaps. Miguel opened his eyes. Then his mother helped him dress and get down the stairs. She seated him at the kitchen table. After he had taken a few swallows of orange juice, he managed to rid himself of his sleepiness. The clock on the wall marked quarter to eight; shortly María Luisa would be coming in to get him and walk with him to the corner where the school bus stopped. When his mother went out of the room, Miguel jumped down from his chair and ran down into the cellar. Without turning on the light he went to look for the brick in the corner. Then he rushed back to the door and switched on the light. With the blood pounding in his head, he returned to the corner, lifted the brick, and saw that the bird was not there.

María Luisa was waiting for him in the kitchen. He avoided her and ran to the living room. She hurried after him. On entering the room he saw the cage by the window, with the canary hopping from one perch to the other, and he stopped short. He would have gone nearer to make certain, but María Luisa seized his hand and pulled him along to the front door.

On his way to the factory, Miguel's father was wondering what he would say to his son when he got home that night. The highway was empty. The weather was unusual: flat clouds like steps barred the sky, and near the horizon there were curtains of fog and light. He lowered the window, and at the moment the car crossed a bridge over a deep gully, he took one hand off the steering wheel and tossed the bird's tiny corpse out.

In the city while they waited on the corner for the bus, María Luisa listened to the account of the proof Miguel had been granted. The bus appeared in the distance, in miniature at the end of the street. María Luisa smiled.

"Perhaps that canary isn't what you think it is," she said to Miguel in a mysterious voice. "You have to look at it very close. If it has a black foot, it was sent by the Devil."

Miguel stared into her eyes, his face tense. She seized him by the shoulders and turned him around. The bus had arrived; its door was open. Miguel stepped onto the platform. "Dirty witch!" he shouted.

The driver started up. Miguel ran to the back of the bus and sat down by the window in the last row of seats. There was the squeal of tires, a horn sounded, and Miguel conjured up the image of his father's car.

At the last stop before the school, the bus took on a plump boy with narrow eyes. Miguel made a place for him at his side.

"How's everything?" the boy asked him as he sat down.

The bus ran between the rows of poplars while Miguel and his friend spoke of the power of God.

Translated by Paul Bowles

Anita the Insect Catcher

Roberto Castillo

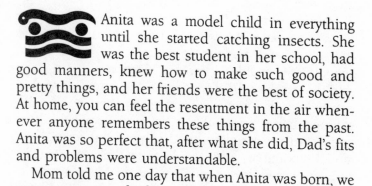 Anita was a model child in everything until she started catching insects. She was the best student in her school, had good manners, knew how to make such good and pretty things, and her friends were the best of society. At home, you can feel the resentment in the air whenever anyone remembers these things from the past. Anita was so perfect that, after what she did, Dad's fits and problems were understandable.

Mom told me one day that when Anita was born, we were very poor, which you have to take with a grain of salt because she always exaggerates a lot. But it is true that Anita hardly had any toys when she was an infant, even though Dad always did everything he could to give her whatever she wanted. At the beginning, there were many restrictions, but my parents were confident

13

that as Anita grew older, the good things would multiply, so that when she was big, she could have the world at her feet. These prognoses were fulfilled with precision, step by step. Anita was lucky from the moment they named her. Dad was consulting the almanac, and it turned out that her saint was Saint Eulogia. My Aunt Eligia became furious when she found out how they were going to name her. She started saying: "What an ignorant man. All due respect for the Saint, but names like that, these days, destroy one's opportunities. Even I became an old maid." They finally agreed that the name Anita was fine because it was modern, it had a nice ring to it, and it was also very Catholic since it honored none other than the Virgin's mother.

It isn't because she's my sister, but Anita had the prettiest eyes anybody had ever seen around here. Everyone said that her deep blue eyes, her blond hair, and the innocent whiteness of her skin made her look like one of those beauties you can only see in magazines that come from the United States.

My parents argued later on, when it was time for her to go to school, about whether they should send her to the school with nuns or to the neighborhood public school. They couldn't agree, but Mom won because she said that in the school with nuns she would develop a psychological complex: "Remember that we haven't stopped being poor—those old ladies only think of money. In the neighborhood school, Anita will be a model student with all the lessons she's received in etiquette based on Carreño's manual. When she's old enough to start high school, we'll be ready to send her to the nuns."

In school, Anita was the best behaved child, the one who always was very clean and well bathed, the one who knew how to sit and talk properly. She also knew how to talk with grown-ups. She was very different from the rest of her schoolmates who appeared lazy, dirty from not bathing, and arrived with sleep in their eyes. Anita represented the school in everything: she spoke at civic activities, literary soirees; she gave speeches and sang beautifully—she was the number one student. Her jealous schoolmates soon started to call her *Stinky* but the nickname didn't catch on because all the teachers were on Anita's side. Even the director of that school would come by the house to pick her up and drop her off after classes.

She had been in school for three years when Dad left the trade as a lathe operator. He started to work with APLAN, which distributed agricultural machinery. There they put him in the sales department, and he made good contacts because he knew how to speak English, thanks to the lessons he learned from the records. We moved and Dad started to pay off the house we now live in. Little by little things started to improve: Dad was already wearing a tie, he bought a secondhand stereo console, and we had a phone. He was so optimistic that, even though he had been so stingy, he gave Mom the record collection called *Latin American Music That Will Live Forever* for Christmas, which was edited by the Reader's Digest, no less. Anita changed schools. She moved on to the elementary school of the Central Academy for Young Ladies, which belonged to the government, yet had a long tradition and prestige. Things were going better.

When Anita finished elementary school, Dad bought her a secondhand piano, and by the time she started school with the nuns, she had already taken quite a few piano lessons. After Anita started high school, Dad became more grouchy, even though he was also probably feeling optimistic. He would say: "Those old ladies only care about money. That girl thinks that only because she's been pampered, she's already the smartest one. Who does she think she is, Miss Universe?" But Mom would straighten him out, talking to him about Anita's great future.

As she progressed with the nuns, piano classes were followed by private classes in English, swimming, cooking, decoration, and embroidery. At that time we had a car, an old Chevrolet that Dad bought in installments from a used car lot. Then, Anita demanded that we join the UNICARD system, and later on Dad bought a share of the Swimming Club. He also became a member of the Casino, although in order to do so he had to persuade a lot of friends and people of influence because they didn't want to accept him even with the money right in his hands. Dad was furious: What did those scarecrows think? Rich people don't even go to that place anymore. Couldn't they see it had gone downhill? Didn't they realize that he had no interest in sucking up to all those stupid old people? Didn't they see that all those old farts, those spoiled old ladies who circulated in that place, that he wouldn't do them a favor even if he was crazy? It's only so the girl will have a half-decent place to get some fresh air and dance every once in a while. Everything was for the girl, not for him.

At this time, Anita's friends were the best around. They never invited her to their parties. Anita would sometimes go with them to the Casino parties but never to private parties. Dad said that it was better that way, that in the Casino someone from the family could always take care of her while, on the other hand, you never know what could happen in those private parties. There are always so many rich and shameless bastards. Besides, you have to see that, even though they don't invite her to their parties, they always admire Anita's intelligence and good manners. *La turquita* Sara drops her off in the car every day; they study together, very seriously, and she even takes Anita in the afternoons to eat ice cream.

Around that time, Anita started to fill her notebooks with pressed butterflies. She would put them in between the pages, and the first one I ever saw had beautiful blue shapes on its wings. Many school girls do similar things, only instead of butterflies they press leaves or flowers. But her own schoolmates became alarmed when they saw the way Anita did these things. They started to notice that she was going overboard, that there was dust from the butterfly wings on the pages of all her books and notebooks. When Mom realized this, she told her to be careful, that if that powder fell into her eyes, she would be blinded for the rest of her life.

During vacation that year, Dad took Anita on a trip to Miami. When they returned, she was already wearing only American clothing; and even *las turquitas* were green with envy, even though they could buy everything they wanted. Dad said: "What a nice trip; we had such a good time. It's fortunate the girl looks the way she does because then those disgraceful gringos won't discriminate against her as they do with those who look more Indian."

After the trip, Dad got more serious with the household expenses: they shouldn't be wasteful because for several months we're going to have to pay the agency for the airplane tickets; we already gave ourselves that pleasure and, as the Lord says, now we have to be frugal. But a few months later, Dad once again gave in to Anita's requests and got more credit. There was new furniture in the living room and dining room, a very decent set of dishes; the front of the house was also fixed up with the addition of a couple of classical-style pillars.

Anita continued being a brilliant student, and there was a rumor going around that when she finished high school, the nuns were going to send her to Paris. As soon as Mom knew about it, she got scared: People say that women over there have a bad reputation. How can I be separated from my little girl? It's good that she's intelligent, but I won't let them make her sick by forcing her to study so hard.

My sister always kept away from the neighborhood kids. But her friends, *las turquitas*, always laughed at her telling her that so and so was her boyfriend. They were extremely cruel with people. They called Pedro, who lived on the corner, "broke butt." Only because he had to work in a mechanic's shop and the monkey wrench would tear the back pockets of his pants, and also because he said "broke" instead of broken, since he never finished elementary school. Also, poor Juan de Dios who worked in the ice cream parlor, they gave him ugly nicknames. They called him "dog face" because of his quite long and canine features. Anita told *las turquitas* that on principle she didn't deal with those boys, but they would only strike back with: "Aha! So it's 'broke butt,' huh?" And Anita turned so red and became so furious that *las turquitas* never teased her again and never again were disrespectful or inconsiderate with her.

In the afternoons, from the school balconies, Anita, Suzy, and Sara would wave their hands at the boys who came to take a look at them. They would pass by quickly in their new cars, or on big motorcycles, and didn't enter the premises because there was a huge iron fence that prevented them from doing so. They would see, while speeding deliriously, the little white hands, beyond the fence on the balconies, waving delicately like handkerchiefs. And from the balconies they were seen making those turns, taking the curves at high speeds, surrounded by smoke and by the noise the tires made while violently rubbing against the pavement.

Anita never got close to those boys, only from the balcony behind the fence. At home, they always made it clear that she wasn't to have any contact with them because everyone knew that they took advantage of the girls who weren't upper class, that they would get them into their cars and then have their way with them. Dad had a fit when he found out how those scoundrels loaded with money referred to the girls who walked along the boulevard on Sunday afternoons; how lucky it was that Anita didn't get involved with those girls. She only went from the house to school and from school to the house; those girls deserved it for getting into those cars.

But Anita wanted even better relationships with our high society people. Dad told her not to rush: "You have to wait a little longer. When you enter the University to study Business Administration, I'll buy you a car, and then you'll really be able to socialize with the best element, and you won't have to ask anyone for a ride."

Around that time, she started to get very quiet during classes. She would have a blank expression on her face, as if looking into empty space. Whenever a mosquito flew near her, she would suddenly stretch out her hand, close it violently and trap it. This was how she collected many insects. Sister Margarita would smile whenever she saw this, and would think to herself, with her lips partially open, *one of God's innocent children.* No one realized that from this was born a habit that Anita would never give up.

Later on, her schoolmates started to comment that when they were at their picnics or enjoying themselves while gossiping about people from their house porches, or while on the beach with their boyfriends, Anita would meticulously examine the bark of the trees around her house. When she finished, she would carefully go over them again. This was how she collected many insects. That's all it was at the beginning, but later on she would perform this procedure with her shoes off and wouldn't stop even if it was raining. She would spend all of her Saturday afternoons looking for insects in the trees, and when it had rained, she liked to bite the bark of the almond trees. But no one became alarmed because Anita continued being the best student, always looking pretty and so well behaved.

Dad continued making better contacts. Now it was common to see him arrive very late at night. He drank whiskey and played long games of poker. Mom had become more and more agitated because she had been told that Dad had a mistress, and got even more upset when a woman anonymously called and insulted her on the phone. But none of this prevented Anita from being the center of attention for everybody. During her last year of high school, Dad mortgaged the house and there were parties and trips for Anita.

She experienced the most extreme changes during that year, but it didn't affect her intellectual performance. She actually displayed an extraordinary talent for mathematics and the natural sciences, to the point that many serious people started to believe that in time Anita could become one of the country's greatest minds. She did, however, become very quiet. No one noticed, but she got too quiet. At the same time, her search for insects intensified. When she caught them, she was happy, dissecting them in a thousand different ways and then throwing them into the corners of her bedroom.

Anita only caught insects on Saturdays and Sundays. But once she had finished her high school exams, she devoted all her time to it. She got a special net and was feverish in her activity. She also started to catch them at night. She would sneak out of her room, late at night, and didn't think of anything but catching insects. She continued eating less and started getting pale. One morning, she jumped over the fence around the house. She was barefoot and waved the net violently and graciously towards the mosquitos, butterflies, grasshoppers, beetles, golden beetles, and all kinds of insects. She was looking for them and catching them near the street, and then she went into the empty lot next to the mango trees. She would bite into the insects she had caught and would then rub them on her face, arms and legs. She returned home late that afternoon with her clothing torn by the thorns and fences; her face was dirty with the insects she had rubbed on herself, and she was trembling, but there was a peculiar expression of happiness on her face. My parents were very scared: What are people going to say? Have you gone crazy, young lady? And Mom: No, it's just that her brain is weak from studying so much.

They didn't let her go out of her room for a long time, but she lifted the floorboards and found cockroaches, which she took out in large quantities. She tied them with threads, learned how to train them, and the cockroaches obeyed each and every one of her commands; they walked to the left or the right, depending on how Anita pulled on the threads. She had teams of harnessed cockroaches. My parents sprayed insecticide in the room and killed them, but she would caress the dead corpses, and they didn't want to take them all away from her at once because she would kick, cry, and act hysterical. She stayed in her room without going out for a few days; she spent her time chasing spiders and lifting more floorboards without finding any more cockroaches.

One day she ran away from home. She was looking more beautiful than ever. She returned two days later, at night. She arrived covered with green grasshoppers and had the sweetest and most sincere smile in the

21

world. She had scratches all over, caused by the thorny underbrush she had gotten into; she smiled constantly and sang pretty songs that no one had ever heard her sing before. She didn't flinch when Dad hit her. She withstood the wild beating as if he weren't hitting her. And Dad: This idiot is smoking marihuana. This is the last straw; this is a decent home and will continue being so; and no one laughs at me just like that.

They got a psychiatrist for Anita. Fortunately, she had already finished high school. No one was excited about graduation because everyone was worried about everything else that was happening. There was happiness, but everybody tried to hide it a little because at home they thought that if people noticed Anita too much, they would spread rumors that she was crazy. However, the nuns gave her a very special graduation gift; they treated her to dinner and gave her a warm farewell: what a shame that this beautiful creature has to go out into the world.

The psychiatrist said she was cured halfway through the following year. She wasn't able to enter the university because my parents said that it wasn't advisable as long as she was receiving treatment. Finally, the doctor said it wasn't that serious, that it was only a matter of a few symptoms of neurosis, which fortunately weren't severe yet and which she had already managed to overcome.

For some months we were at peace. Anita was talking again, she slept well and ate quite a bit. One day she escaped but returned in the afternoon, and my parents said: "Poor thing, she just needed to go out, and it wasn't anything serious because she didn't come back with any insects." These outings continued, but the household was peaceful until the day when there was a rumor going around that Anita met with strange friends at the parks.

One time she was lost the whole day and arrived home very late at night, with her clothing torn. Dad was furious and couldn't control his temper. He started to hit her, and Mom said: "You don't have to hit her, she's still sick, my poor little girl." And Dad, talking like a madman, answered: "This isn't a matter for psychiatrists. What this idiot needs is a few blows to learn once and for all; this will be her medicine."

After this, she was strictly forbidden to go out. But after a few days of being locked up, Anita convinced Mom to at least let her go out to the yard, that she would die if she continued indoors, and she started to cry. And Mom said: "My poor, precious, little girl, now you have to be good; you can go out but you have to behave." And Anita had barely stepped out into the yard when she made a dash, leaped over the fence, and went running into the street. Mom screamed hysterically: "Come back, Anita, don't be bad, I love you so much. When that man comes back, he's going to kill me because he's going to say that it was my fault." And she continued screaming until she lost sight of Anita.

She was gone for four days and, even though the police were notified, couldn't be found anywhere. On Saturday morning, she appeared, barefoot, wearing a pair of blue jeans that obviously didn't belong to her because they were too big. She came in singing, without saying hello to anybody. Her face and hair were covered with mosquitos, and she was smeared with blood because she kept squashing them with her palms, as if it were some form of entertainment, and the blood from the insects dripped down as it mixed with her sweat.

This time, no one said anything to her and they didn't even hit her. They just washed her and told her: "See what you get into? After everything we've done for you, and you're so ungrateful. How embarassing. Don't you see that we still owe the psychiatrist money?" Anita didn't respond; she only continued singing and looked as if she had come from another planet. Dad got drunk for a week and was also acting crazy. They sent me to live with Uncle Carlos and Aunt Loca for a while—at least until everything was put in order—so I wouldn't be the next one to go crazy.

Now Anita spent her afternoons singing sad songs. She would sit next to the fence, which she couldn't jump over anymore because she was being watched too carefully, and she never lost that strange smile she had when she returned from her last escapade.

A few days later she started to vomit, and then they discovered that she was pregnant. Then Dad couldn't take it any longer: She can go to hell, that whore. This is all we needed; now she's really finished us off. And Dad kicked her all over, and Mom had a nervous breakdown that resulted in an unpleasant tic in her lip that they still haven't been able to cure.

Anita lost the child she was going to have. It seems that some friends helped her for a while after she was kicked out of our house. But she ran away from there too. I was very small then, even though I remember quite well. However, some things I did learn afterwards. At home I can't talk about this because Anita was never mentioned again. Since all of this happened, Mom spends all her time in church and attending charity meetings. Dad, embittered, continues drinking and getting into more debts.

Of Anita, all I've known is that she got very sickly. She had typhoid and looked emaciated, and because of this, she was unrecognizable. They say that on the banks of the rivers which surround the city, she sticks her hands into the sand, searching for crayfish and worms, which she later gives to the fishermen. It seems that for a time, the kids in those areas would chase her, scaring her, and when she would start to run, they would yell, "There goes the *siguanaba*." But this must be pure talk.

Our house changed so much after what happened to Anita. It feels as if even her memory doesn't exist anymore. As for me, well, the truth is that everything is going well. Dad understands me quite well, even though he never cracks a joke and never confides in me. Recently, he got it into his head that as soon as I have my fifteenth birthday, I'll have to attend the Military School.

Translated by Cynthia Ventura

Confinement

Horacio Castellanos Moya

Third day of confinement. I guess I'm no longer used to it. I feel a kind of tightness in my chest, as if facing these four walls were a bad omen. I wish I could go to the movies, walk down any street among people, take in the sun, breathe in this city that has always been my vanquished enemy. Nostalgia is a slightly sweet variation of sadness. If I had a good book, then maybe things would be different, but the *compa* says there aren't any books in this house, only a moth-eaten encyclopedia that's not worth the trouble of bringing in to me. I'll have to make do with the newspapers.

At this time of day the heat has already subsided. I can distract myself for a bit by looking out of the only window in the room; it opens onto a small patio made of cement and is crisscrossed by clotheslines. I've been given strict orders, however, to close the blinds when anyone approaches the patio. That makes this dark room even more depressing.

Soon it will be dusk; I can tell by the light breeze and the flocks of squawking parakeets. I would like to see the sky, especially at this hour. At any moment they'll knock on the door for me to pick up the plate they've left on the floor. My appetite, that's the only thing I haven't lost; I've been on too many marches and suffered too much hunger on the war front.

I'd like to know where I am. It's not that I want to go against the rules, but it wouldn't be right if in an emergency I didn't have my bearings. I wish Javier would come by so I could ask him. The last time I saw him was three days ago. He picked me up in a van and told me to get down on the floor. They were going to keep me in hiding for a week because things were getting tough here. I haven't seen him since. Only this *compa* that's taking care of me. He's always well dressed, looks like a professional. I don't like his wife's voice, it's very aggressive. They don't have any children.

I wonder what Fina is doing right now. I can imagine her having dinner, quietly, with her large eyes, staying close to her rifle. It would be enough to just see her, to have the chance to speak to her once in a while, even if she were suspicious and distant. My heart must be like a mound of earth full of unsprouted seeds, it's all desire.

It's a quarter to midnight. I wrote two poems. I was going to describe how the enemy ambushed us as we returned to the camp at Palo Grande, but when I picked up the pencil, the only thing that came out was a quivering melancholy, allusions to my loneliness, to my confinement. I tore them up, of course. How long has it been since I've written a good poem, one that I like? At least three months. I tear up everything I write. I tell myself that I need to distance myself a bit, to find some peace and calm. But is that possible in the middle of a war? Even when I've traveled outside the country, I have had so many things to do I don't get a moment to myself. And now when I have all the time in the world to examine my memories and emotions in depth, everything I write seems tedious. What a contradiction. Something has snapped in my relation to poetry. Maybe if I read something stimulating . . . How long has it been since I've read a good book? Since my last trip to Mexico, about four months ago. But a guerrilla is always on the move, and I was forced to leave Cendrars's complete poems behind. Shit. All I managed to read was "Little Joan of France" and "My Seven Uncles or the Panama Canal." How my life would change if only I could get my hands on that book or another like it. But I shouldn't despair. Everything in its own time. Maybe my problem is my haste. I should be patient, let my experiences gather, give them time to settle; it's no good to try to vent them all at once. Of course, for that to happen you've got to know where you're going in life. Maybe that's my problem.

I feel trapped, not so much by fear or desperation, but by a strange presentiment, a more or less nostalgic state of being. Maybe it's the sudden uprooting from a given reality. The last two times I left the front there wasn't any need to confine me. How I'd like to have a drink. I'd sleep better, especially in tonight's impeccable silence; you can't hear any shots, or any cars going by. The only thing I feel is a current that starts in my chest and ends in my throbbing temples.

I started the day with a letter. I told my brother Ignacio about my poetic misgivings of last night. I told him that I envied him in Mexico where he can get good books and immerse himself in the right atmosphere for writing. I asked the *compa* here for an envelope and to do me the favor of mailing the letter. Before he left I asked him to bring me a couple of volumes of the encyclopedia. It's the *Barsa*. I never thought it could so take my mind off things. Had I known it, I would have spent my time reading something useful. It's already midday, and I haven't even finished reading what I find interesting in the first volume. It must sound strange to go on like this about an encyclopedia, but this is the first time I haven't had plenty to read in confinement. I remember the two weeks that whisked by in a sympathizer's house in San José, Costa Rica. She was a literature professor, and I felt like I had a short scholarship just for reading. She had the whole Casa de las Americas collection, impossible to get in San Salvador. I read every issue. Or that other week that whizzed by in the San Jacinto hideout. There was an archive there with almost every document of our organization. But this is the first time I've felt incarcerated, without anything to read, all on account of my prejudices. And all along there was an encyclopedia at arm's length.

It's hot here. I'd feel good if I could keep some ice water on hand, but I don't want to bother the *compa*'s wife, whom I don't even know. Besides, she hardly says a word. She only knocks on the door to leave my food or to let me know that I can use the bathroom: she says "you can go now" and hurries into her room. Whenever I hear her move about I think of Fina. How do I always manage to fall in love with difficult women? All the men in her squadron are after her. What's worse is that she's in the infantry and I'm in logistics, so who knows if we'll ever see each other again. This morning as I was taking a shower I felt like masturbating in her honor. But I felt bad. Whacking off in the bathroom at twenty-seven is lamentable. Celibacy is the guerrilla's calamity; you can't do anything about it.

Nearby, a church has just tolled its midnight bells. I feel at ease, like I did when I smoked cigars on my parents' patio under a full moon to while away the hours of insomnia. I've been rummaging through my memories; if I could live my life over again, I would live it exactly as my instincts have dictated. I didn't join the revolution on account of poetry, as our maestro Roque did. I joined the revolution out of instinct, like the tiger that sniffs out its prey. It's only those who are afraid who have to do intellectual acrobatics in order to join. That's not my way. I think of Ignacio struggling against time, questioning himself, intellectualizing. Me, my instincts put me right in the middle of the battlefield.

I've given some time to thinking about what war means to me. It steels my spirit, sharpens my nerves. I wouldn't be anywhere else. Ignacio calls me a "sober fan of danger." I'm a fan of life, in my own way. I'm not searching for ideals or engaging in conceptual struggle, that's not what war is for me. But it *is* a battle of wits. The gringos on one side, with all their arrogance; and we on the other, ready for anything, feverish with reason. There's no other explanation as far as I'm concerned. Bloodshed? I don't celebrate it, but it gives me certainty. It runs very deep. Extremism is our life's only guarantee. But it is a lucid extremism, I don't lose perspective. We couldn't have asked for a more formidable enemy. It's not up to us. Shit, this night has gotten too heavy for me.

When he brought me dinner, I spoke a while with the *compa*. He's all right. We chatted for half an hour and verified the watchword. I concluded that if the beast descended on us, we'd have slim chances of getting out alive, and if we did, it would be in the worst manner, putting up no resistance. There aren't any weapons. All I have is the watchword. I explained to the *compa* that under these circumstances I need to know where this house is situated. He told me he had no authority to make exceptions to the rules. But I insisted, and he took a sheet of paper and drew a small map on it. Then he folded it and gave it to me on the promise that I'd open it only in an emergency. He told me I'd know my way around with no trouble.

Last night I dreamed that I was walking along España Street, in San Miguelito. The enemy had surrounded the area. Two tanks were blocking the corner of the Fausto movie house. I was coming down the sidewalk alongside Maria Auxiliadora School when a Cherokee without license plates and full of the enemy drew up and idled alongside me. I clearly remember the screech of the brakes. My heart began to pound so violently that I woke up. What a relief. I spent fifteen minutes tossing and turning in bed before I fell asleep again.

I've just had a great supper. The *compa* brought me a pizza and a beer. He even gave me a book. He told me he knew nothing about literature, but as he went by a bookstore downtown, he remembered that I had asked him if he had any novels. He got me a copy of *The Red Badge of Courage* by Stephen Crane. According to the jacket, it's about the gringo civil war. I'll have something to entertain me tonight.

The *compa* also brought me some good news. Yesterday, we launched a new offensive. In Chalatenango Province we occupied Tejutla; in Morazán Province we're about to take Jocoaitique. Things must be really going well. It's too bad I'm not allowed to listen to the radio, but the house next door belongs to ARENA spies.

I wish I could go out onto the street, listen to passersby's comments, get the feel of the place. A bus ride is the best way I know of gauging a city. A murmur in the crowd or the slightest expression on a face is enough to determine the impact of the war on the city.

As soon as I get authorization, I'll go to my parents' house. They steer clear of politics but are totally immersed in the everyday life of the city. Through them I'll find out what people here know about the war, the rumors about the enemy's failures, how our own forces are advancing. My poor mother, every time I think of her it gets me down. Luckily she's calm and doesn't make scenes when we say good-bye. But deep down it's probably worse. She controls herself, but I can see the anxiety eating away at her inside. She has to take all my shit without a word. My father is another story. Nothing fazes him, as if he didn't care what I did or what might happen to me. But deep down he probably feels the same as my mother, only he plays dumb. I don't know why I'm thinking of them now.

It's two in the morning. I've just finished reading Crane's novel. I liked it. It made me think of the many things that could be said of our own war. For better or worse I'm only good for writing poetry, and with poetry you can't say all these things. It's strange for me to think of the gringos having ever been heroic. But that's precisely why I liked the novel. It made me re-member—or better still, value—my emotions in the middle of a bombing. I've had little combat experience. I always wanted to be transferred to the military units, where you get the taste of gunfire and learn to savor it, but when the *compas* ruled it out, I resigned myself, rationalizing that logistics needed more level heads. Who knows, maybe it's all the same.

Today has been one of the most depressing, somber days. I tried reading the encyclopedia or rereading Crane, but I wasn't able to concentrate. I spent the day in bed with my eyes fixed on the ceiling, tracing pirouettes in order to control my thoughts, more to give some order to the mountain of dispersed, useless images. I resorted to the adolescent habit of retracing the guiding thread of my ideas, recuperating the past bit by bit, but it was to no avail.

I've been thinking that confinement—the practice of confining the guerrilla—has a remote precedent in the three days that Jonah spent in the belly of the whale. Solitude, understood as a form of confinement or even imprisonment, could be understood as the starting point not only for great mystical or religious experiences but also for great political adventures. "You're repeating very old ideas," our maestro Roque might say.

If I were an orderly, systematic person, I would take advantage of these days to take stock of my life. But for that I would need to plan my life, set objectives, goals and schedules. Is there such a person? I can't evaluate anything because I feel adrift, like a cork floating on the tide. But my life just rides the current, depends on the organization, that is.

A few minutes ago the *compa* came in. He told me that Javier would come get me in an hour. I asked him if I was being transferred because of a security problem or if they were releasing me. He didn't know. It feels good to leave this room, this guinea pig's life. I'm happy, ready to dive into the city. It's like being born again. A good thing.

Translated by George Yúdice

Story of the Maestro Who Spent His Whole Life Composing a Piece for the Marimba

Mario Payeras

Patrocinio Raxtún went into the jungle when he began to get old. Originally, he was from the region of the *guarda-barrancas* birds and the *palos voladores*.* He left that world because all his material possessions consisted of three orange groves spoiled by time. He knew how to play the marimba from childhood, but the daily preoccupations of worldly goods exposed to the vicissitudes of light and to the voracity of the migrations left him no

*Poles used in an ancient Mayan dance.

time for music. Searching for happiness, he spent long weeks descending the humid slopes of the Cuchumatanes mountains, entering deep into the boisterous universe of parrots in the rainy season.

By the time the torrential rains had stopped, he had arrived at an old village, on the banks of the Chixoy River, where no one seemed to be living. Life passed by in the shade of the big *sapodilla* trees. There he fixed up an abandoned house, scraped clean its sprouting beams, and organized an economy inaccessible to the laws of trade and to the predatory species of the air. The band of monkeys, who from their solitude spy on the affairs of men, saw when the mouse-eating boa, which until then had occupied the house, slipped imperceptibly away.

As soon as he had taken care of his material needs, the maestro began building his marimba. He didn't want to return to the birdless solitude of death before having ordered in time the melancholic mathematics that kept him awake. He knew that in the jungle there are favored varieties of wood that can become percussion instruments, thanks to intellect. The construction of marimbas is based on ancient equations that allow man to transform the material of which morning glories are made into a matter of intelligence. So, with the arrival of the season when the parrots create an uproar from daybreak on, Patrocinio Raxtún went into the forest in search of the *hormigo* tree. It is a sonorous species which, despite its passion for rain and its canary's calling, makes the ax reverberate. It took him two days, besieged by swarms of bees that turn the salt of ordinary physical labor into sweet forms of energy, to chop one tree down and separate a piece large enough to obtain twenty-six keys.

What followed next was the work of light and time. The piece of *hormigo* shed its bark; the wood absorbed the sunlight and expelled from its tissue any chance of new flourishing. In September, when he hit it with his ax head, the wood had the resonance of an empty bottle. Then the maestro placed the plank on two sawhorses and, under a sky filled with magpies, started sawing until he obtained a piece wide and thick enough for the marimba keys. Following the grain of the wood, he cut out twenty-six pieces of diminishing proportions, measuring according to an ideal model that in the world of tangible things would take up three-quarters of an arm's length. With the rough work done, he applied himself to the precision work of shaping the keys.

There is an exact relationship between the age of the wood and the timbre of the sound it produces. But the sonorous quality also depends upon the volume of vegetable tissue under the mallet's blow. Thus, with each piece it was necessary to plane away any thick sounds to the ear and to calculate positions from memory until obtaining the material equivalents of a scale measured in thought. The musical value of the longest key he fixed arbitrarily, taking as a reference the lofty sounds of reality and then reducing them to everyday dimensions. When this first key was ready, the sound it produced was similar to that of the swollen raindrops on the tile roofs of the *altiplano* in May.

He was figuring on finishing the keyboard in December, but unforseen events complicated the project. The years of contradictions, contending with the thrushes and sparrows, had deteriorated the aerating tree inside him. While he worked on the tenth key, his ribs started to ache and he was left short of breath. For several months he remained prostrate on his makeshift bed, feeling himself turn rapidly gray. But the sickness developed in his organs a new form of wisdom. His body became sensitive to the slightest

changes in temperature, and his bones could forecast
the dews. With extraordinary precision, he was able to
chart the itinerary of light on the complex map of
spring. Each morning he made an inventory of the
damage to the finished keys caused by the routine
processes of matter. When the winds began blowing
from the latitudes of the whales and pelicans, Patrocinio Raxtún realized that any possibility of making
music depended on the capacity of his tissues and
those of the *hormigo* to resist decomposition. In May,
however, death's migrations suddenly abandoned the
tree of life. A few days later, he was again working on
the marimba.

While he was convalescing he finished the keyboard. Twenty-six wonderful keys, tied in a bunch,
awaiting a musical intelligence to give them the definitive order they would have in the kingdom of objects.
With the discretion of one who knows he is surrounded by a fragile, transitory world, the maestro
proceeded to build the weightless, patient frame,
where parallel strips of gut would support the keyboard. He fitted it with two legs and attached a seat to
the structure, so that the whole thing called to mind the
figure of an equatorial beast in the zodiac.

In a part of the loft beyond the reach of the creepers,
he had tucked away from the previous rainy season
three dozen gourds, a resource used by old musicians
to resolve the problem of resonance. Under each
key he placed one of these recipients of sound, in
an order determined according to their size and
sound property, as the acoustic virtue of each gourd
may not always correspond to its dimensions. There
are corpulent gourds with delicate resonance, and
there are those with deep, booming voices capable
of echoing the roll of thunder and the thunderous

clatter of rain, whose size and shape don't correspond to the power and intensity of the sounds. Hence, the unpredictability of the resonance system in simple marimbas. To obtain music from the humble instrument, only rubber-headed mallets were lacking, a traditional way of softening the blows to the docile wood.

After three years of living in the jungle, Patrocinio Raxtún began to play. On sunny mornings he would place the marimba under the *pito* trees in the patio and devote several hours to exploring the keyboard. He realized it was going to be difficult to express the delicate matters of the *guardabarrancas* birds and of the fireworks on an instrument of uncontrollable resonances, better suited to convey the atmospheric clamor of the multitudinous parrots in the realities of deluges and immemorial springs. What he attempted to capture had to do with the wild tails of spinning kites that trace the Great Bear in the immense night sky of the *altiplano*, with the sadness of the iron cocks on rusting weather vanes, with the invisible pathways of the birds. These were simple, exact things transformed, nonetheless, by the wood into torrential rains. That's why he avoided simultaneous sounds and sought to produce clear, sharp notes.

He began the piece with a slow sequence that lingered in G, so that anyone listening would know it spoke of things of the past, suggesting a lamentation for their absence. Next, he played a rapid C to gather momentum and then, very slowly, released all the nostalgia of his ephemeral meanderings through time, alternating high and low notes whose synthesis and combination evoked December's vast stars within arm's reach, the geraniums in April, the brief life of the blackberries, and the fleeting happiness of the caged canaries carried by roving fortune-tellers to the fairs. When all this was said, without haste, without accelerations that might confuse some things with others, mourning a bit for the precarious elusiveness of time, he added a brief passage with the mallet in his left hand, which began before he finished the part he was playing with two mallets in his right hand. It spoke of pleasant, though fleeting, things. It alluded to the occasional dances of the Moors, that remain forever in a world of mirrors and swept patios, celebrating masks with perfect teeth and cruel smiles, moustaches made of melted gold, blue gazes and ecstatic expressions of the Christians under a foreign sky filled with *cenzontle* birds and *palos voladores*.

Through the music, he showed that it had always been this way, that happiness consists of having seen and being able to remember, and that the world resides in memory's unmarred wardrobe, free of dust and unchanged. Time and again, he would say the same things. He seemed to repeat the previous point exactly, but, in fact, each narration reflected distinct facets of the soul. He realized that the order and movement of the music shares many of numbers' customs, that music is a mathematics of emotions, and that numbers that flow are necessary to express the movement of things in the spirit.

Playing the same piece over and over, Patrocinio Raxtún didn't sense the definitive arrival of old age. More and more often he fell asleep under the *pito* trees in the patio. In April, he came to the conclusion that all his music would last less time than a sudden downpour. When the rains again arrived, he brought the marimba inside and shut himself in until the storms would pass.

His body sought out his makeshift bed, his spirit remained in the remote reality of rainy season parrots.

The musical instrument suffered the fate of common objects. The rain seeped into the house with the days, and the humidity of life crept up the legs of the marimba. Months later, the wood sprouted new shoots. In October, a mouse-eating boa slipped into the house to live.

Translated by Richard Schaaf

Guatemala 1954—
Funeral for a Bird

Arturo Arias

Máximo Sánchez crawled into the light. He had been hiding with his mother under the big old desk. Now that the bombs had stopped, he could see the world. He wanted to see the things his mother had told him about: elephants, houses, spiders and streets. Maybe he would hear someone call his name, and if he did he could answer. His mother had told him this, and his age too. He was five years old and already knew so much! Well, he was four and a half in truth, but Máximo felt bigger if he said five. He said so with scars on his cheeks. They were scars from something called welts. Everything had its name. Máximo went through the zigzagging streets, between the ruins of the houses. He looked for everything, and its name.

There were bodies all around him. These were called corpses. His mother had told him not to touch, because they were filled with nasty worms. He had asked his mother if there were worms in him too, but she said they were just in the dead. Poor little corpses. He wanted to play. It was a pity they were dead. But they stank so much! They deserved to die for smelling so badly. He continued to walk with one hand over his nose and the other over his belly. And his father? Would he smell too? No! His father wouldn't stink. He wasn't dead—only maybe. His mother had told him that his father had disappeared. Maybe now that the bombs had stopped, his father would return. Máximo remembered his father's handsome mustache. Will you come back Father? Soon? Will you come back?

Máximo could walk in any direction unless the streets were blocked by corpses or fallen walls. That was called freedom. But the air wasn't free of the stench, and this freedom had its limitations. He lifted one foot, balanced lightly on the other leg, and leaped, arms open, over a puddle of blood in the street. Despite that, everything seemed possible. To fly, to float, to wash, to run here, to run there, to run always. He felt free.

Then it began to rain, softly at first. One drop followed another, with plenty of time between one drop and the next. He could feel each drop caress his hair, and see their explosions against the remains of the old walls. Inside the drops he saw red and blue colors. Drops crisscrossed and absorbed yellow until they touched the grey dust ground. Then they ran together in colorful furrows, and grew like a spider's web. Where was Father? Playing the spider? The drops fell more forcefully, falling without end. Máximo got cold and wet, pursued the colors, caught shades of marine blue spilling behind violets. He ran through the streets, goose bumps forming on his skin instead of welts. He passed smiling corpses, mouths open, and feared they would bite at his heels. His mother had told him they wouldn't move, but Máximo wasn't sure. He studied a cockroach scurrying from one of the open mouths. Were they born inside a dead person? How would they know when they were born? Something struck him on the forehead and fell in the mud.

A bomb? He searched for it and found something like a cold piece of glass that melted. More of these began falling on every side. A big one hit his shoulder. He had to find a place to hide. It was cold. It had never been cold under the desk. He hoped his mother would still be waiting there with her white hair and toothless mouth. Would she still be bent? Maybe he ought to go back. Then another hit him. And he went on without knowing its name. Maybe he ought to go back?

There it is! Look at it!

He was in a very narrow alley. In its center, there was a dead bird. So he was not the only one! Children of all sizes were there shouting.

A dead bird! A dead bird!

He had never seen a bird, dead or alive, except in photos from old magazines at home. He had looked at them all the time. This bird was smaller than he had imagined it, silently crossing the sky with bombs under its wings.

A dead bird! A dead bird!

The children ran toward him, and he ran too. He didn't see the headless body behind the pile of mossy bricks. He stumbled on it and got his belly full of mud. Blood dripped from scratches on his arm, but he didn't cry. Instead, in a fit of anger, he kicked the corpse, his foot sinking through the body as though it were a cotton sock. Corpses, corpses at every turn! Then he remembered the bird.

Look at it!

Soon a circle of children surrounded it, and the eldest watched that no one got too close. Careful there! Don't step on it! Brutes! One of the littlest boys started to cry. But Máximo wouldn't do that. In sepulchral silence, the eldest kneeled, facing the body. Poor bird. He touched it and trembled. Murmurs. He extended his middle finger to stroke its tiny breast. The murmurs grew. Someone pushed through the group to see, and stepped on Máximo's foot. But at this moment, only the bird mattered. Poor bird. Let's touch him too. No. Such a delicate body would be torn to pieces. Poor bird. Its rounded breast was covered with dots white and soft as the drops of rain. Its wings pressed down around its body as if in protection from the cold. Its neck was long, almost too long, and ended in the head where a big black eye and open beak protruded. Stiff feet stretched directly upward. You think the hail killed him? No. When something hits, it leaves marks. Look at what the bombs did. But this is different, bombs explode. Why should this be different? They kill don't they? Yes, but they kill differently. Maybe he broke his neck? Maybe. The eldest crouched down, and carefully took the head of the bird between his forefinger and thumb. He lifted it a little. Everybody bent down to be able to see better. What are we going to do with him? He laughed, already knowing they had to bury it. Of course, everybody shouted. We must bury the bird. Poor bird. Máximo saw the beautiful bird, as he had seen the colors fleeing from the dead walls. All the birds were gone.

Everyone ran towards the ruins to look for objects for the funeral. Máximo didn't know what to look for. He had never been to a funeral. He hadn't heard anything about them. He had seen pictures, but wondered what a funeral could be. The eldest said they should bring pretty things, but Máximo knew he couldn't grasp the colors. Nevertheless, he searched for something, something that glowed, and he began to dig through the ruin closest to him.

Beautiful things. I only want beautiful things!

One of the boys brought a board. Another brought a colorful cloth. One found a picture of a rose. A tall freckled boy rang a silver bell. Someone had tallow candles. There was a watch. An oilcloth slipper. A medal from the air force. Two pairs of pants. A yellowed laundry ticket. Máximo was the last to arrive. I found a ring! A precious ring, he shouted. The circle of children parted so he could pass and place his offering at the feet of the dead bird. He was proud of his discovery. And it was truly precious. Solid gold with a delicious aquamarine mounted exactly in the center. The finger it encircled also seemed beautiful.

Was it the finger of a woman? Look at the fingernail. Maybe. But it isn't painted. Some women don't paint them. Maybe it's a Martian finger—it's half green. No, that's because its rotting. It isn't rotting, it's only half burned, if it were rotting it would stink. Perhaps then it would smell good? You haven't by chance smelled a corpse, ever?

"Okay, enough," said the eldest. "We have to bury the bird. Is everyone in agreement? Good." With everyone pushing for a good view, he crouched before the body and gathered it up in cupped hands. He put it on the board, and some of them applauded. "Good. Now you cover it with this cloth," he ordered, "and we'll put the insignia above the head. Like that. The great dead pilot. Put the ring at the feet, finger and all. It's the finger of its owner."

The freckled boy with the little bell led the procession. Stopping on each corner, he rang it shouting, "There is a dead bird! A dead bird!" A line of pious boys carried candles and followed the photograph of the rose held high in the air so that everyone could see. Two boys hung the trousers on pointed sticks like flags. One brought the golden crucifix without any body. The board with the deceased, carried on the shoulders of the six eldest boys, came next, with the youngest children, Máximo among them, scrambling into the rear of the line. The rain continued falling. But the bird was dead. They would have to bury it in the rain.

They decided to bury the bird by an intersection in a vacant lot. The youngest ones dug the hole with sticks, the oilcloth slipper, an old broom. The land was soft and moist, and in almost no time at all they had a large enough hole.

The trousers were put in place at the bottom. On top of them, the photo of the rose, face upward. And after that the board with the body and its precious adornments. Everyone stood in a circle around the grave, with their eyes fixed on the lifeless feathery body. The only movement was the murmuring rain. The oldest boy took the crucifix and let it fall on the body. Good. Cover it. All at once, they dug into the mud, each trying to throw more dirt than the others. No one saw the old man who approached.

"Children, hey, you over there! What's going on?" They all whirled around. Máximo saw the old man, black coat dragging in the mud, legs bent and half useless. He was leaning on a wooden stick, and there was mud and food on his filthy gray beard. His pallid skin was covered with splotches of welts, especially on either side of his broad nose. His jaw bone shook.

"What are you doing?" he asked.

They stood there paralyzed, afraid. The smallest one cried again. Another one ran away. Soon, very soon, there was an avalanche of boys pushing, elbowing, scratching, all to get away from the place as fast as possible.

"Don't leave! Don't leave! I just asked what you were doing!"

Máximo was the only one left. He scrutinized the old man. Could this be his father? No. The old man had no mustache. If he were his father, he would have a mustache. This is how he had always seen him in pictures. His mother had also mentioned that the gringos had no mustaches, but his father did. He wondered why everyone else had run away. And this old man—why were his hands trembling? His feet twisted? Why did he have hair in his ears? Should he have fled also? Maybe the old man only wanted to talk. Why should he be scared?

"Hey there little fellow! Will you come here?"

Máximo was scared. "I have to go home. My mother is waiting for me under the desk."

"Don't worry my boy, this old man isn't going to hurt you."

"I have to go. It's simple."

The old man shouted to the other boys. "I see you! There you go! You act like rats scurrying around the ravines. There—by the Street of Illusions and Street of Sighs."

Máximo looked. Street of Illusions. Street of Sighs. For the first time he realized that the streets, like people, have names. Máximo had a lot to learn.

"By the bones of my grandmother!"

The old man hobbled over to Máximo.

"What were you rascals doing here anyway?"

"A bird died. We were burying it."

"A funeral for a bird?" said the old man.

"Yes. We found it on the street and couldn't leave it there. It was so beautiful and soft. Someone might have stepped on it."

"Of course. Did you find it on that street? The Street of Sighs?"

"Yes, that one. Then we decided to bury it here. We dug a hole in the dirt and put it inside. Then we covered it."

"You did this and nothing more? You didn't leave something to accompany it and to protect it from the cold?"

"Yes we did. We had a procession, and gave it a ring and a medal of gold."

"Well, you made an effort, but this isn't how to bury the dead. Of course, it wasn't your fault. I'm sure none of you have had experience in the matters of death. But let me continue. When you have the bird on the board, you must burn it with incense. Then sprinkle the body with flowers of death and some drops of *indita*.* This helps the soul on the road to infinity. Of course, these days you couldn't have located any *indita*. But you could have improvised. And there's one more thing. When you lift the board, you must give three turns to the right and four to the left. Seven in all. This is to confuse the soul so that it can't return to this life of misery. Imagine if the poor thing had to live life all over again? Of course, you wouldn't understand." The old man opened his mouth to laugh. But nothing came out of it.

Translated by Ann Koshel

---

*Guatemalan Spanish, meaning "small Indian woman"; also the name of a strong drink, said to have an "indita" in the bottle.

I Am René
Espronceda
de la Barca

Leonel Rugama

to Doris (María Tijerino Haslam),
great admirer of César Vallejo.

In general, I never got through a difficult
and challenging school assignment without doing a lot of work, and the more
complex and intricate the readings were, on all sorts of
subjects, the more I threw myself into it (—René, know
what's playing at the movies today? René, don't you
know what's playing at the movies today? I wanted to
go, but I didn't have the time, and Silvia told me it's a
beautiful movie, that it's one of the best films with
Manrique Canal and Grieta Pardo, and also Parles

Geton, Ticher Burlon and Sortija Flores are in it—), and I knew how to come up with smart answers, since it didn't matter if it rained or thundered, if they talked about me or not, if it was hot or cold, if it was wet or dry out, or if it was sunny or cloudy, or if the day started out soaked in rum or scorched by the sun, or if the rainy season never ended or it had subsided, or if the sky started to clear or if we were in Indian summer, or if the girl who drinks chocolate milk came by or not, or if there were huge windstorms like when the Devil boldly walks around during Easter week, or wild blustery winds or gentle breezes, or sudden downpours, or endless rains that washed the streets clean, or if hail fell or fishes, the way they once fell on the doorsteps (also around Easter week) and my uncle used to go around picking them up, sunfish and catfish—that's what they loved to call them—almost always rained down.

Or the World News blaring on the radio and all day long the soap operas or the year's top ten on the *Hit Parade* with singers singing full volume, and the kids playing and racing their little cars and screaming as though their throats were going to burst, or if our neighbor's radio was on a different station, also turned way up, or if our neighbor on the left had tuned in his short-wave to Radio Havana and it's also blasting and the broadcaster is giving the news about the sugar harvests or the latest kidnapping or about the next amateur boxing championship or Fidel talking and giving a speech about intellectuals or the Second Havana Declaration, or "Liberation movements will not disappear, for as long as there are people who are exploited, there will be men who bravely know how to grasp a gun" and all the transistor radios blaring and in the kitchen Argentina is washing the plates and the plates are banging against each other, or she's washing the spoons and the spoons are clanging against each other, and the noisy scouring brush or the toilet just flushed, or the rice sizzling or the beans bubbling or the coffee boiling, or the clothes being washed and scrubbed and pounded against the washboard and the sound of the water pouring off like a waterfall or rapids, or the sound of the soapy suds gurgling down the drain and more noise when it occurs to Argentina to sing.

And the noise from a big truck going by, raising a big cloud of dust and the dust flying all over the place and getting all over the house and dirtying all the furniture and my clothes, and my shirt collar is filthy and so are the sleeves and the kid's clothes, and Argentina sweeping the dust and raising another cloud of dust and the raspy voice of doña Joaquina telling her that it's better to spread wet sawdust on the floor because it keeps the dust down better and while she says this she sneezes and then Argentina sneezes and Argentina sneezes again and she saying, "Damn, I'm allergic to dust, but René apparently doesn't notice anything when he's wrapped up in his reading."

Or the Coca-Cola truck making a big racket with all the purple Fanta bottles and all the clear red Milca bottles rattling and fizzing up, or the ting-ling-a-ling-a-ling of a man who's selling ices or a man yelling "Snow-cones! Snowcones! Snowcones!" and the scraper scraping the ice to make the snowcones and then he says "Here you are" and the squeaky wheels of all the carts and wagons, and the peddlers yelling "Fresh vegetables! Fresh vegetables! Fresh vegetables!" and another "Coal! Coal! Coal!" "Firewood! Firewood!" "Popcorn!" "Bread!" "La Preeeeeeensa! La Preeeeeeeeeensa! La Preeeeeeeeeeeeeeeeeeeeeeensa!" "Shellfish!" "Pork! Pork! Pork!" and the ting-a-ling-a-ling-a-ling-a-ling-a-ling-a-ling of a man who's selling fresh fruit with milk and containers of chocolate milk, and the "you son-of-a-

53

bitch" of one boy towards the other, and "your mutha" "she's yours" "the old bitch" "that lame-brain" "the one who throws away tortillas" "that fat slob" "cheat" "you know who" and the voices fade away little by little each one going their separate way.

Or the sound of a boy who goes by scratching the wall with a stick and from time to time stopping and writing "asshole" "pussy" "prick" "faggot" and he continues moving on, scratching the wall with his stick and shouting "Drop dead you ugly bastards! Drop dead you ugly bastards! All of you, all of you, all you ugly bastards! Me, me, me . . ." and it would fade away and then one more time the shouting and the scratching on the wall.

Or two boys walking down the street and shouting and tossing a ball to each other and the bargain-seller barking "Exciting! Dynamic! Exciting! Dance for the benefit of Jesus the Crucified" or "Big raffle for a luxury car for the benefit of the Consecrated Tomb" or "Attention ladies and gentlemen! Attention ladies and gentlemen! We are here to let you have for the ridiculous sum of one small peso, for one córdoba, listen up good to this offer we're making for the ridiculous sum of one córdoba, one small peso, a peso, that's all, one single peso is next to nothing, you sir, you madam, you young man can take this marvelous, yes sir, yes madam, yes young lady, you can take this incredibly marvelous and cheap set of kitchen spoons for the ridiculous sum of . . . and here comes a nice young girl, yes, fine, and for one small peso the young lady has decided to take this marvelous and necessary set of spoons, you too sir, madam you as well, you also young man can decide for yourself and stick to it, for the lousy sum of one peso, one córdoba, now that's not sky-high, one little peso doesn't make you rich, doesn't make you poor, yes young man, what will you have? What can we get you?

Good, now he's getting away with only paying one córdoba national currency for this marvelous wonderful set of kitchen spoons, attention! attention ladies! attention ladies!" and the loud noise from a motor bike that zips by backfiring and leaving a big cloud of smoke behind or the longslowanguishing sound of a bleedingredracingambulance or the squealing of a car peeling away fast and whipping around the corner like a gangster or the same car slamming on the brakes to let Jorge's son cross who's chasing after his ball and he's only a little shaken up, but if something had happened to the kid, Jorge would've gone nuts because he's always drunk and doesn't notice, and the one thing about Jorge is he loves his sons and whoever doesn't like it has to face him, and he's the kind of guy who . . . I remember when he (Jorge) kicked a servant just because she gave Roger (when he was little) a tiny scratch, and that was on her kneecap.

Or the noises sounding very far off and the kids in the square giving the woman who's always screaming at them a hard time. And not all the transistor radios blasting, not all the kids shouting and yelling, not all the trucks, not all the street peddlers and not even Argentina's grating voice can pull me away from my *fascinating* readings "The Truth about Dogmatic Theology" "A Year by Year History of the Development of Industrial Metaphysics" "Commentaries about a Trip Beyond the Grave" "The Most Famous Crimes" "Damned to Distrust" "The Folly of Eulogies" "Sand in the Blood" "The Rebirth of St. Francis of Assisi" "A Powerful Group of Theologians Congratulate God on His Naming" "The Death of Jesus with an Epilogue and Appendix of the Stages of the Cross" "An Atheist Contends That There Are Three Different People and One True God" "The Almighty" (authorized by the Holy Father of the Church of Leon XIII) "The Song of Songs" "The Martyr of the Segovias" "The

Way of the Cross" "The Ultimate Magic of the Word" "Astrology" "The Divine Oracle" "The Problem of the Birth Rate and its Repercussions on the Last Judgment" "The Magnificent Prophecies of the Virtuous San Malaquías" these titles are in my latest notes on what I'm reading, that's right, and I remember I've read some other things and it all adds up to about twenty thousand famous biographies and close to five thousand famous poems and various secondhand anthologies of the most famous poets in the history of the world, and the complete works of the theatre, leather-bound, and written on very delicate onionskin paper. And on top of all this, I always keep up with the great source of information in the newspapers, paying principal attention to the literary and cultural pages.

Moreover, I must confess I cultivate the letters in my free time, devoting myself to composing the most finely honed verses, and not all the pandemonium in the world can get in the way of this work.

But today, after two months of being separated from Argentina, who left with all the kids because of certain extremely private problems, today I find myself totally cutoff—or at least in good part cutoff—from the maddening noise of the city which I find bearable, but here in one of the most isolated barrios in the city, here I'm beginning to go crazy in places where the silence is almost profound, which is an excellent quality but I don't need it, and it's not unbearable either due to my large capacity for adapting, that's right, at this very moment I'm beginning to go crazy, slowly, little by little, and then all of a sudden I go nuts without even time to wonder where my agony is leading, or if my craziness will be peaceful and if all the volunteers in the barrio will take care of me or if, on the contrary, I'll be a wild madman posing a big threat to the neighbors and if I'll decide at any minute to throw rocks at the front doors of all the houses or at the churches which is much worse, or if it dawns on me to take a bath and I don't come out till the Judgment Day, or, still worse, if I go to the john and sit there for a long time and nothing happens and I leave as satisfied as though I had done something, or I decide to tie my shoelaces in knots so tight no one will ever be able to get them out, and I go walking around here with them like that till I drop from exhaustion or I wear down the heels and even the soles, walking around strung out, on the edge, in knots (of course, I mean the shoes) or else never opening my mouth, not to eat or anything and spending year after year like that or poking my eyes out and staring at everybody with empty sockets and spitting at the first guy who makes a wisecrack; but something I've always been afraid of is going outside naked in the street, and stark naked like that all the folks in the barrio tie me up and bring me to the madhouse under the pretext that I'm crazy, that I've lost my grip or I've sprung a leak and then, even worse, they leave me there among so many strange nuts, when you don't know who they are, much less where they're from or what they're like, if they can take a joke; and actually what I'm scared of more than being tied up or brought to the madhouse or finding myself among so many strange nuts, is that they leave me in that house, the one I hate so much, because ever since I was little I sang in the church choir and always I wanted to throw something from the altar, because there was a strong angry odor and a stench of unbearable shit up there that was mixed with the foul smell of the crazies and some old withered flowers that they had placed on the altar.

Well, tonight I just barely started reading the newspaper when a fly wouldn't let me have any peace, and when I was reading "an unfamiliar but always present page by Vallejo" the fly again landed on my head as though it was licking my hair, and I threatened it with the newspaper and it took off towards the candle "THE INTELLECTUALS (again I feel the fly on my head and I'm ready to give it a good swat and again it flies off towards the candle) AND POLITICS."

The artist is, unavoidably, a political person. His lack of purpose, his lack of political sensibility, should serve to demonstrate spiritual barrenness, human mediocrity, and aesthetic inferiority. But, within this setting, must the artist become politically active? His field of political action is multiple: he can vote, he can protest, such as leading a group of civic-minded people, like from any barrio (and now the fly is buzzing around my ear and flying around my head and buzzing around my ear again, and now worse, it's landed on my ear and has started to walk around in there, well, a good whack ended that and now it's circling the candle and I can't see a thing from staring at the light, and it's driving me crazy and I'm starting to get a coughing attack and the fly manages to land on my neck and is walking around my collar and the coughing's getting worse—enough already! and now I'm so afraid of spitting on the floor and this spit in my mouth pisses me off and the fly continues its trek across my back, and it bugs me, so to speak, when insects go for long hikes on your skin, so I sit up and try scratching my back when I notice that the fly is trapped in my shirt and this is a relief, because now I can decide the fate of this damn louse, and though I feel a little queasy I'm driven by necessity and the miserable time I'm having, so I try squashing it between my back and the chair—I think I got it, ugh! and I think I can get almost any disease from squashing an insect so full of germs), he can lead a doctrinal, national, continental, radical or universal movement along the lines of Rolland. In all these ways the artist can, certainly, serve in politics; but none of them answer to the powers of political creation—creating, by preference, inquietudes and political nebulas peculiar to his nature—and none of them end up being more than anyone's catechism or collection of formulated and, therefore, limited ideas (but if the same fly that I killed on my back is again on my hand, and worse, sucking me dry and leaving a wet ooze right where I hold my top, ugh! disgusting! and I already shooed it away but the damn fly came back and now it's dancing right in front of my eyes trying to get in them, and up my nose, and maybe I should just leave it alone and let it bother me, but it keeps chasing me and I feel the uncontrollable urge to cough and powerless to spit and that fly won't leave me in peace, and I wish I had two mad-dogs or *lagartija* lizards or *pichetes* (three different names and one true animal) so that the two of them would swallow it up in one gulp, and damn this cough- ing and I have to make myself get up to spit hawkers out in the backyard because of the same stupid fear of spitting on the sidewalks just because it's not my house, and the fly lands on my head, on my foot, on my hand, on my back, on my face, on my ear and it tries going up my nose, in my ear, in my mouth, flying buzzing around, around my head wanting to land on my mouth on my eyes again trying to get in my mouth again going for long walks across my back, shitting on my tongue, walking around in my lungs, nesting in my stomach, buzzing buzzing buzzing, walking on my face on my mouth on my nose) if the artist gives up creating what we could call the political nebula radiating throughout human nature—reducing it with propa- ganda and proclamations from the barricade itself to a secondary, sporadic sun—who then would be touched by that great and wondrous spirit in all of us?

Translated by Richard Schaaf

For These Things My Name Is René

Mario Roberto Morales

How do you suppose he was going to be (his face blurred as though another one behind him, even more identical, was about to appear) with that hand of yours like a connection to the return to begin again (in its every instant), and to the afternoon air, now like the breath that inflated your chest and staved off the threat of its being burst like a carnival balloon at which a kid is about to squirt a brine-filled water pistol and scamper off. Or worse yet, like the final burp of that life David transmitted with his hand, arm, and fingers, which began to stretch out to you long before they were within reach. His way of saying How are you? always had a meaning that was lost between the habitual smile and the legs and battered shoes entering the car quite slowly, easing a hip bulging with a .45 onto the seat. He would sigh, symptomatic in people whose lives are fulfilled, you were thinking (even though he was only twenty). Rather than exhaustion, he seemed to be expelling plain, ordinary carbon dioxide from his soul. All in all, it was preferable—and today you know it's so—to be asking yourself how it was going to feel to see your hand now out of your control moving toward the ignition of the station wagon to reinitiate fear once again (your reason for living) and the return to begin again all that made you feel alive, the absence of which tells you that you don't make sense out on the street without a .45 just like David's stuck in your belt.

How were you going to feel if that route had to end at a certain location each day, and each day it threatened to end with your chest caved in by rifle butts? That's why the street—that one or the one of the contact point—was no good and never had been any good except for just this: to show you the terror aroused by doing that for which you thought you were born, but before its time. So, better do me the favor of explaining to me in clearer terms how you felt, instead of calling up your memory of all the times he got into your car— one of the few legal ones—and about the uncertainty as to whether today we are just going to talk, *compa*, because that bomb won't be picked up till tomorrow; and, of course, his not being there, the eternity of his slow-moving legs, and the climbing into the car that seemed never to end.

But you dwell on the recollection of that facility of his for slipping around corners and leaving you alone with your admiration and your ignorance instead of telling you why. Besides, he'd lost his ID while in the getaway from an action, and you had seen him precisely at the moment he was making up his mind not about whether he should go totally underground but how to. Whatever the decision, he asked you to hold something in a paper bag for him while he tied his shoelace. It was in the weight of that wrapped-up regulation pistol that you found the way to being what a man should be under certain circumstances and in a certain place: your own. And then also that casual way of taking you to another *compa* who was living for good in a sweat-shirt, and telling him nothing except that everything was okay, that he mustn't go near his house, that they would meet later at their contact point, and that he would try to get him some clothes. And then he said to you, "Well, we'll be bumping into one another in an action one of these days, and from now on you'll be working with this other guy. *Ciao*, take care." And that was the end of the experience with David—or whatever his name was—and the last news of him until his appearance in the papers—disappeared—and the mulling-over of that recollection began what hadn't hit you before because you were getting your teeth into something new every day.

David would always give the impression that his wind-breaker and the bulge under his faded shirt were permanently part of his skinny body, that they had been molded there from a model for heroic deeds, and that unquestionably he was going to die before me. It's the impression of dryness seen in faces accustomed to sensing death every day in best-loved eyes. And even though I also went through a stage of being absolutely without tears, I was never able to be a David or a Pedro (who, I believe, is still alive in prison).

So many anecdotes that time cast in mere feelings! There they are, a bit touched up, you'd say, by remoteness, although the creeping sickness of wanting to take part in every action would have led you into addiction, you know, to the ignoring of feelings, to the impasse that caused you to waver, not knowing which was colder, the metal of a gun or that of the cap of a pen, or that the ultimate achievement might be turning corners

63

and killing military police in cold blood. But that's another story that still lurks behind the eyeteeth of so many dead friends. *What matters now, and has mattered since last year, is opportunity instead of silence, anxiety, and not that anxiety which won't go away because of the anxiety that keeps it from going away, the cold of the night, anecdote and not anecdote dissolved in the heart and in the throat choked up for want of shrieking; action, fear, life, and not its damnable, insurmountable memory.* All this will come about, my friend, but not by magic. I now know that it must be built. You knew it from the first time David settled his legs on the front seat of the station wagon and your life started on its headlong course toward death.

I used to say How are you? to him every time he got into the station wagon and accommodated his legs on the seat, the bulge of his .45 then showing all at once under his shirt like the volcano at midday or a peasant's hidden quarter-pint. The passage of crumbling doorways, the drivers with averted eyes, and the music on the radio made me think of the village, of that backwoods village, yet not so backwoods that it could escape having them pave its streets and aspiring to the category of city. I refer to the village in which the revolution—today a thing of fear, afternoon, and Peugeot—would be transmuted into my arm holding up a rifle.

Yes, but tell me something: How do you suppose that man was going to be if today you yourself are convinced that life has a macabre capacity for taking an absolute nonentity from grave to grave and making it possible for him to do what he did (one blinding hot day that recalled those past) in the way he did it—with no merit whatsoever—and to be as great, while being as full of fear, as the others in that bit of afternoon, which turned out to be a bore for those clouding over the rusty gates of the cemetery with their cars. I know it wasn't your fault that you're alive, but those metallic willows of the cemetery, the continuous arrival of everybody entering through your windshield, and what was evoked for you in the rearview mirrors, tell me, Whitey, that you're pleased. Deep down it makes you happy, and leaving the movement was one of the best chess gambits of your life.

The thing is you don't realize—and that's lucky for you—that there are moments when you can't determine exactly whether the shadow of the trees that lets thin rays of light reach your adipose outlines is bearing witness to the acts of a failure or a fortunate man, which translated into your jargon implies the possibility—or impossibility—not of dying, but of getting to be a doctor. But you're both, Whitey. On the one hand you're in school, and on the other, the Hippocratic Oath has already poisoned your mind with that line of drivel that justifies scholars like yourself to not be on the streets slugging it out with the police. The point is reached at which you don't know what kind of failure you are, particularly when you slowly approach the little garden where Robles's smooth skull lies—*filaria*, you think—whose marble stare makes you realize that you are, in fact, both kinds of failure. But that's too much for your conscience even though you can understand, I'm sure, that you'll never attain the dimension of life afforded by having your genitals in the right place and not for having treated them in accordance with the most elementary principles of hygiene, which if followed by the people would mean less venereal disease and, who knows, possibly even reduced infant mortality. Yes, Whitey, there are two doorways to the recovery of human dignity, and you've been granted passage through the smaller and more pusillanimous one, and, let me tell you, the distance from one to the other is the same as that between heaven and earth. And don't, under any circumstances, try running through my ABC's for me. I too settle everything here on earth. Yes. Here at the roots. Here, where we have a sense of history. Here, where those of us who already know before we die of the never-ending leaden rains being unleashed over the peace of graves and for that reason are already dusting off epitaphs.

Ah, brother, only militancy can give you that feeling of being greater than the enemy; and to think that the effort of recapturing the valor of that first time has been arduous, that the previous time was always erased by the one following, and that all at once your life is crudely smeared on the pavement if it so happens that life doesn't deign to leave you alive to make every effort to evaluate what is already beginning to hark back to the past in a kind of prior priority, to become a stage and not an event. But all in all, you must remember that those situations often go on right where they are, although René—"For these things my name is René," he said to you on leaving. "And what's yours?" and you thought Sartre and told him Juan Pablo—is still making a contribution to the revolution and you don't walk at his side anymore trying to see through the reflection on his huge eyeglasses.

Now we're beginning to recapture that first time, do you realize that? And, let's face it, René was really far from being a David or that second contact he left you with at the cemetery entrance that afternoon. Only René knew how to talk to you—well, all of them knew, my friend, all of them—how to introduce that bourgeois bulk of yours, your concept-infested brain, and your social sentimentality through the narrow aperture of revolutionary consciousness and—why not say it—the rest of the slogans with which they had to replace your altruism and decency. It's true; don't say it isn't if you are able to admit it. You felt the walls of the fancy shops shake and thought that the bus windows were watching you—and would be spitting tear gas at you any minute—because they knew you weren't standing on that corner waiting for a girlfriend or contemplating the passersby like the other students, puffing up your self-image. You were expecting that classmate who insisted, when he'd be drinking, on talking to you about the movement. You were waiting for René without yet having met him, and all at once there you were walking beside him because your companion had disappeared in the crowd. A contact has been made, you said to yourself, and under the very nose of opulence.

Although you were far from feeling satisfaction that night, you considered your own life for the first time, an instant before walking into the coffee shop with René. But it's destructive to think of today's tactics—let's not discuss kidnapping, because that's a piece of cake now—without taking the ones we aren't familiar with into consideration and whose value is evident from the fact that contacts were being made not in the poor sections nor in hovels nor hash houses but at cocktail bars of the sort that seem outrageous to those doing the fighting. Let's repeat that he said to you, "For these things my name is René. And what's yours?" Juan Pablo, you answered. You felt a sensation as though the neon lights had flavors.

And that first time begins to stretch thin like chewing gum, because even though you went home skipping, skipping all the way like a school kid just let out of an exam, an unpleasant, didactic aftertaste persists that slips out into the dimension given you to fight in and thereby to have a chance to die. You would never have thought it possible to imagine David's shoulder blades—again entering the car—like two hooks out of an old, old museum of the revolution that was commencing today at four in the afternoon from the Peugeot's black dashboard with its radio at low volume. Here you are out on the streets, beginning to eat up the miles with a pleasure that stems only from an easy conscience and the smoothness of an excellent set of tires at the service of the revolution. The revolution that would come about one of these days because you were being told so by the afternoon, by the sun beginning to strike the frames of your dark glasses, by the contours of the car, and by the sensation that the rearview mirror was a kind of sensor gauging for you the degree of its achievement. Ah, yes, morning is garish for revolution in remembrance—but only when remembering those spells of bad conscience. There, revolution is afternoons and clouds that you'd be imagining over your village, silent and enduring, where the tension of waiting for David would be transformed one day into your right arm holding a rifle on high. All of that was the revolution in the calm of the street corners until David himself showed up dragging death after him in his slow pace, which was the revolution in those spells of bad conscience. How far removed David seemed to you from the glory of collective awakening. He is under sentence of premature death, you thought. *He wanted to kill because he had never done so before, and it may be assumed that he died with a taste of curiosity on his smashed lips.*

That way you had of answering unemphatically was taken for simplicity, your avoidance of direct glances as righteous, stored-up anger; it was all nothing but fear, though, Whitey, which you so badly need now when you know you won't be feeling it in the same way because the defeat of existence has enabled you to look them in the eye.

I don't know why it was, but David always had a dead look. He would appear around a corner with a book covered in newspaper under his arm and with his smile. It was something in his eyes, his dry skin and its scaliness that bespoke the imminence of complete death. He always walked slowly but gave the impression of a slab of steel, upright, ponderous, and sure, walking toward the bullets, toward the afternoon, toward the night filled with police, but with the certainty that he would not fall ridiculously to the ground, ever. He would fall slowly . . . his eyes remaining open; and once dead, he would continue beside me in the silence. He would materialize on any street, on any afternoon he saw me around the corner, hugging the walls, in the dust that I tread along the boulevard or in the damn diesel clouds of the buses. There, once more, would be his wounded presence forever in the memory.

I hadn't yet met him at the time he went up into the mountains. He was there for six months. It was when he would tell me about the experience that I began to suspect that this twenty-year-old boy who read Mao while he stood waiting for me on street corners, this smiling kid with the dry skin, had a perpetual yen to massacre people in uniform.

That's normal, Whitey. When you finally come to terms with the option of struggle, your life turns into the life of a militant, totally tied in with one faction at war against another. Then, yes, brother—when your life no longer has value, is no longer a commodity belonging to your parents—then, yes, the dormant little bug of blowing away your fellow men who interfere with the people's progress, awakes; and that's what was happening with David. He thought of the military cadres, who do nothing any longer but make war, who've gone totally underground, with no ties to family or the hope of even walking down the street until power is taken and oblivion; to those guys, brother, soldiers look like piñatas.

One afternoon when he was on duty—he said—he saw an army patrol approaching along the road in a ravine, and he set up the machine gun—a tripod type—but the commandant ordered him to hold his fire. The soldiers began disappearing like lost fruits, slipping away silent and green, smoothly as serpents, into the undergrowth. His fingers trembled against the chill of the machine gun. It was going to be his first experience, and they had frustrated it.

You were a witness to the second frustrated opportunity. It is enclosed by a chest of drawers and a white little bed, a lamp and a faint sobbing, the mirror, that mirror you left behind when you kissed your wife and the baby, and couldn't say what you were going to do, couldn't give her to understand that you might not be able to return. You looked at the room for the last time, thought of your son and of the memory they will have formed of you in this jungle of evil tongues. You went out into the cold of Avenida Elena. You imagined the hand coming down over the palm trees that were once there and beginning to crush out your memory. It must have been the heavy clothes and unseasonal weather and, in addition, possibly, having the capacity to discover the dialectic like a malignant ant in the diapers of children and ascendant in the clear, star-studded December sky. They emerged out of the night, David's cautious footsteps and the purposely hidden face of the *compa* who was waiting for him on the corner and had no reason for you to know him. The parked automobile (at a neighborhood movie, according to your mother) would be useless, Avenida Elena useless, after a lifetime of painting houses with bitter whitewash, stripping the leaves off the palm trees, attaching mercury lights to their trunks. How was he going to be—here comes your usual greeting once again—if he was coming back frustrated a second time.

His face was a blank except for its usual inexpressiveness, no anxiety in his glance other than the remote reflection of two glass shards dulled by the light and the smile and the hand outstretched before, long before, coming within reach. "The action was postponed," he told you. At once, the talcum powder and your son's irritated little ass were back in your nostrils again. You saw the station wagon again parked in the garage in its slot (you thought) and again imagined climbing the stairs to the second floor and your wife's creased belly, and the disappearance forever—for that night, at least—of the image of the abandoned station wagon and you yourself done for, doubled over the rearview mirror on the door, pouring out your blood uselessly, mourned by only a handful who, though of one's race, one's flesh and blood, one's own people, were not exempt from the vulgarity of being counted.

If David could have known of your swinish sense of relief, he would have blown you away then and there (I exaggerate), and if you could have known of his frustration, you would have analyzed it that night in the solitude of the room and the silence of your wife and child. But that night was not so remote from either of you that you could be thinking about it. To live one night, my friend, is to penetrate not so much its obscurity but that which lights up inside yourself thanks to such darkness. Things may or may not transpire in the night, and whether they transpire or don't, life always transpires, gnawing at people's insides, licking at them, wearing them away, putting an edge on them, sharp and not at all regular, as the sea does to reefs with the very blandness of its water.

Life, like the sea, is eternal, friend, and transfixes you no matter what happens, or what doesn't ever happen. You see how wave keeps weaving into wave if no resistance is put up to the hoarse murmuring of the past. You see how things begin to emerge, sometimes in inverse order to that in which they were dropped into the drawer of memories. . . . Because once and for all we must get out the pistols and the automobile, and stand on our own feet, even though props of a more specific kind are required to hold up a body as shattered as yours. Nevertheless, your hair, your blonde mop, gives you away, having made of you, then, the

71

same you as always, which is what liberates your body, because you forget life to begin living. You live in the face of a future that no longer wants to be encumbered with those plans, with that fleeing, with those two military police who weren't even going to have anything to do with it anymore—absolutely nothing—with the screams of those people running away when David, Davicho, little David, put four bullets into each policeman in the middle of their chests.

Sometimes, however, life snuggles in, makes its nest in the pit of the stomach and undermines the mucous membranes, making them stretch and fold in on themselves, and it dwells there like a tapeworm that must emerge from its dark paradise. It's hard to swallow more, because that embedded parasite devours everything, and you begin dodging and circling it like a clever but inexpert karate fighter, waiting to spot its weakness. A careless move, an opening, and from deep inside, the prolonged, endless vomiting begins to come on. You grab hold of a pole, and you keep bringing up your guts the whole length of Avenida Elena, and you track it even further back toward the corner of Calle Doce and Sexta Avenida, where David's little red car was to wait held up with clutch and accelerator, never the brake. To where David would come racing over, weapons flung in first through the fly window, the others in after. . . . Now you'll never know who the third one, at the wheel, was going to be.

Why did they throw me out of the organization? Is it that they were putting me to the test those times when actions were suspended at the last minute? I believed that the time we were supposed to pick up a car and distribute flyers was going to be another of many that would also be suspended. I realize I'm talking like a coward. . . . And that time I said that I wouldn't go because—I lied—my son was very ill. The truth is I was the sick one; by then my nerves were playing me too many nasty tricks. I told them I couldn't and that was that. When they—three of the compas*—left me and were a distance away walking slowly alongside San Sebastian Park, I felt myself emerging from a long cowardice and going into elemental torture. I had always been afraid of saying I wouldn't go, but that time I was able to say it. My fear was too strong for me. After that David disappeared (his photograph and real name appeared in the papers) and my breakdown reached its low. The days and nights went by in uncertainty, until, inexorably, class serenity set in, class contradictions, class remorse, equivocation, words . . . and class poetics. Everything became fused in a golden crucible, and life's blows blended together forever—or at least for a while. René, Pedro, David, victory or death for Guatemala . . . the Rebel Armed Forces.*

Yes, Whitey, he was a *guerrillero*, wasn't he?

Whenever I think of David—or whatever he was called (his name was Antonio Roberto)—something strange comes over me. His face lies inexorably at the bottom of many things. I think the clipping of David's photograph is still inside a book of his I never returned to him: Socialismo *by Georges Bourgin and Pierre Rimbert. I don't know where I put it. I saw it one day at my mother's house. I was sitting in the green armchair in the living room and read that a student of the Instituto Central had disappeared. Then, I was overtaken by a spell of meditation, of opening files, because a place for him had to be found in memory, and put in order, where he could be left to sleep, so that he might come out on the streets once again, afterwards.*

You knew him but never had any special feelings about him. He was just another *compa*, that's all. *You're making a mistake.* They blasted him when he was twenty years old, studying for his bachelor's at the Instituto Central. And he was a *guerrillero*. That's all. What else is there to say?

Translated by Asa Zatz.

April in the Forenoon

Julio Escoto

Dawn broke and General Fernández gave a jaguar leap on the army cot, making the hemp covering, soaked with the sweat of a night of fever, slip onto the dirt floor. He got up and immediately felt the pain in his jawbone sinking its slivered tentacles into the area of his wisdom tooth. He lifted his hand to his face, but instinct halted it in midair. Willingly he lowered it to his waist to check if he was still wearing the field revolver he had slept with during the night of silent twitching, watched over by the anxious eyes of aides who gathered together beyond sleep and the suspicion of death. Inside the leather tent the scent of human odors lingered, mixed with the fertile aroma of mint ointment, and a yellowish haze of dust glowed against the motionless sides, held there since the last appearance of the sun.

General Fernández stumbled slightly in his riding boots, having trouble keeping his balance between the suffocating vapors and the first gasps of an early awakening loaded down with sultriness and thirst.

"God damn it," he said, thinking about the bugler as he walked to the entrance. "They forgot reveille, the sons of bitches."

At the entrance to the tent he pushed aside the mosquito netting and lifted up the dust guard. A wave of light and the smell of salt invaded the small space, spreading out over the empty ammunition crates, the wash basin covered with a scum of mosquitoes, the field maps rolled up under their tin cylinders, and the saddle with silver rivets and lignum vitae stirrups resting on a sawhorse. A dusty locust took three leaps and flew fleetingly by his face; the general spat onto the pasty wrinkles of the plain, streaked with volcanic silica, that opened up under the heels of his boots.

The first thing he saw in the distance under the waxen April sun, which was laying waste to plum trees and shrinking beehives, was the reddish dripping shape of his three field pieces, rising up with their backs to the mountains and their sights aiming at the tent where he had spent his penance chewing on a wisdom tooth wrapped in poultices of tobacco and lime. When he got his eyes in focus, loosened by the fiery sheet that was engulfing the plain, he saw something he had never before glimpsed in the erratic wanderings of his most intimate nightmares: he was alone. They'd left him alone on the dawn of his day of glory, the eve of the final battle, facing the execution wall of his own misfortune and under the now withered trappings of the mirage of power. There was no word for it. "Damn it to hell," he cursed, scaring off the iguanas nesting under the army cot, and picked up a repeater rifle with his groping accordion-wrinkled hands. A dirty trick like that couldn't be played on the president of the republic, and he pulled off three good shots at the pine wall. "Swine," he muttered, his throat all choked up with a furious custard of indignation.

After the shots the aides came running in a hurry, still wrapped in the pink dawn of morning, pulling up their pants, adjusting their suspenders, hastily putting on their goatskin leggings in a watery cloud of rising dust that patted them on the shoulder, whitened their mustaches, made them sneeze. Commander, they said, boss, what's up, just tell us, but the general looked at them from the distance of misbegotten mistrust, you bastards, weren't you aware of the general desertion, take another look at the military husking we've been put through, where did you leave your hopes while you were asleep, soldiers of the nation, he stuttered, trying to speak, an enemy that's too light-footed for lead soldiers, never, Gen'al, I swear by the virgin, Gen'al, what happened was that you got careless and they stole all the eggs out of the nest while you were sound asleep and left us singing in our tents without soldiers or weapons, artillerymen taking a walk, sentries running around, lazy's what you were, it couldn't have happened, Gen'al, they'd reform the army right then, capture volunteers, enlist peasants, go out and convince the deserters to come back.

"What's the problem, *compadre?*" Colonel Sanabria came in, his spurs jingling, as he buckled his belt. General Fernández looked at him again with aroused feelings, in that cordial distance between both men there was an electric current of suspicious energy. Although there were family ties between them, and although they'd taken part together in previous campaigns against the guerrillas—the same trenches, the same women, the same wealth from the state—their two ambitions couldn't fit in the same room. Both had the mutual virtue of sleeping restlessly and letting their watchfulness bog down, inventing friendly withdrawals for each other, affectionate steps backward, diplomatic rivalries. In their protocol embraces the warm splendor of an assassin's love always glowed, for whose use and advantage they had been endowed by nature.

Seeing him and having the stab of the molar return happened at the same time for General Fernández. Turning his back on him—even with him behind him the general sensed the frigid look of that colonel with the body of a proud bull, run through by three bayonet thrusts in the Acajutla uprising—the general quickly opened his tobacco tin and took out two pinches that he mixed with a touch of lime and then put into the hollow of his mouth, settling it there. He softly tightened his jaw without lessening the look of pain, least of all in front of his *compadre*, and he slowly felt the dampness of the mass placed there and the corrosive taste of the tobacco juice that was bathing his gums. The placid warmth was making him give off a spontaneous gush of saliva, wetting his mouth and making him kick harder.

Colonel Sanabria was looking at the bullet holes that had bloomed on the pine boards when General Fernández came out with a curse.

"Cowards," he said with clenched teeth, a brace of diamonds of hate gleaming in his eyes, "just like when we were fighting in Zelaya gulch. They all ran out on us, scared of the enemy."

"We've gone through bad times together," Sanabria added without seeming to judge the weight of a double meaning, "but we survived. That time we came out on top too, so I haven't got cold feet, *compadre* Mr. President." He patted the general on the shoulder. "I'll get them back for you right now, that is if you'll give me a little time and permission to shoot a few of them by way of an example, like the other time."

General Fernández only answered with a shrug of reflection. The other time it had been via a ministerial decree and by his own hand. But now, was Sanabria trying to get one up on him in public opinion? If he gave in, it would be he, Sanabria, who would appear as the upright follower of regulations, after all, that was what was the most important, regulations, in the eyes of the lawyers in Congress; if he disapproved, the guerrillas could come and find him without any weapons, without any men, without any power. The colonel seemed to be reading the swirls of that secret thought in the air.

"*Compadre*," Sanabria explained softly, with the conviction of someone with all his cards on the table, "we believe what we want to believe, but reality imposes itself."

"There you go with your historical foolishness again," the general interrupted. The exclamation dislodged the wad of tobacco. He curled his tongue backwards and put the rough lump back in place. "This is no time to go thinking back to the Greeks again," he chewed softly. "Get going," he ordered. "I'll give you three hours to put the reins of another army into my hands."

Colonel Sanabria clicked his heels noisily, stirring up a layer of dust that eclipsed the gleam of his spurs. He went out, touching his revolver with his fingertips, seeing the walls of the tent out of the corner of his eyes. Outside he was engulfed in a sudden salty burst of sunlight.

"And turn the cannons around, *compadre*," he still heard his *compadre* shout. The colonel smiled with pleasant rancor. *God damn them*, he thought. *Those deserter bastards have even got a sense of humor.*

General Fernández flopped down, done in, onto the old army cot, an inheritance left him by the last intervention of the marines. Was the heat getting to him or was it the fever coming on again? He unbuttoned his shirt and opened his uniform; the gust of hot air, smelling of tobacco, made the hair on his chest dance, but he turned his face away with repugnance at his own breath. *Anyone who chews tobacco*, he thought, *is only a step away from eating shit.* Smoking wasn't permitted in his presence, or drinking; a theosophist couldn't allow bodily relaxations that rotted the brain. His government had reached a reconciliation of spirit and flesh, but it had been hard for him to reform the habits of Indians, teach them the gifts of obedience, the acceptance of peace. *If it weren't for the guerrillas*, he thought, *with their bombs and attacks over four years, resisting the civilization we were giving them, what a sea of tranquility we'd have had.* In the sixteen years of his being in charge they'd been the most dangerous of all who'd dare raise their hands, challenge his reasons of state with liberal talk of elections and individual rights. Could they possibly know what an individual was?

He sat up and with a couple of tugs opened the laces of his boots, then he went over to a corner of the tent and began to thumb through a bundle of folders, notebooks with stamped documents, copies of decrees and resolutions stuffed into leather pouches and cotton satchels. He put the little mahogany box with his decorations and braid to one side. Under an exquisite blue album, decorated with delicate sketches of doves in flight, he found the medical cups. He picked up the album and with a breath blew away the film of dust that was beginning to settle on it and form a crusty coating of volcanic earth. They were his love poems, his secret voice written only for the eyes of two people, his chosen one and him. Tenderly pondering that hidden vocation, he felt his heart and molar pain him at the same time. He picked up the porcelain medical cups, pouring the colored liquid from an opaque jug into them as he held it up to the light, and he walked about, tripping over ammunition boxes, pouring the liquid from one cup to the other and breathing in with desperate gulps the oxygen that came from the pink bubbles and purple bulges.

It was true, he could see, calmer now, that there'd been bad times, but long good stretches too. From the two attempts on his life he hadn't suffered any misery, even though he still had a lingering taste, a small glow of sensation because of the poison put into the drink with which he was toasting at the banquet—a lack of elementary conspiratorial good manners, not letting him finish that dinner of sumptuous quail and steaming pork tamales. The other one didn't even merit the reminding scar: hiding a stick of dynamite among the candles on his birthday cake was an act of unfortunate vulgar imagination. If the chorus had lasted a second longer and if he hadn't blown out the candles with such strong lungs, he would have been blown to bits, his atoms mingling with the ice cream trim and the rice pudding. That was an offense to his dignity, and he'd rather forget it. Even so, the flight of the conspirators had been such after the failed attempt that he had to classify it as "trips abroad" in order to shut up the foreign press, always ready to see the hateful manias of a dictator in his acts.

What did they know of his civilizing function? Only his *compadre* could understand the grandeur of the mission they had undertaken, in spite of his tiresome liking for Greek history that made him pull the pedantry of his famous quotes out of his sleeve or take on the gestures, posture, and mimicry of a tropical tragedian. "Beware the ides of March," he would say: the clown, not realizing it was a Roman ballad. But even if it was a fluke, his foresight impressed me. After the San Miguel revolt, "You have to negotiate," he advised the general.

"Negotiate? You're crazy, negotiate with the rebels! Whose side are you on anyway?" he'd accused him.

"You have to negotiate," he repeated; "there are a lot of them, thousands of them, *compadre*." The general was on the point of having him arrested, thrown into the dungeons of the central castle, when the colonel added discreetly, "It will give us time, *compadre*, it will give us time to send in troops and place cannons on top of the lookout and blow them to kingdom come, make mincemeat out of them." Sanabria rubbed his hands with malicious delight.

During a week's bombardment of the city, the colonel punctually sent him a rose for every hanged rebel, with brief notes that proclaimed the brotherly faith with which he was defending the Constitution. "You're a brute, *compadre*," the general joked, receiving him on the steps of the cathedral for the victory parade. "You've wiped a whole city off the map for me, you're an exterminator."

"I'm the instrument of God," the colonel had answered, chewing on the words under the dry wrinkles of his military weariness. "I'm your right hand, *compadre*, nothing but a toy for the forces of destiny that you manipulate." The two embraced, weeping, under the approving look of the bishop and the heap of roses that overflowed the altar.

General Fernández heard steps outside the tent, the movement of recruits, neighing, and the bustle of equipment. "They're coming back," he predicted, "little by little, but they're coming back."

After the San Miguel uprising, however, he'd been forced to loosen his hold on rewards. Congress asked his permission to award Colonel Sanabria the highest decoration, the National Condor, making an exception to the death-in-combat clause, of course. The sleek lawyers trembled with emotion over the audacity of their initiative and from the pleasure of his presence, which enfolded them in an atmosphere fraught with intense animal charisma. That was the first time he really thought about the notion that filled his dreams: Give his *compadre* the high Order of the Cedar Cross, but post mortem. Then that swarm of ball-breakers came asking him to reach even higher than his modest emotions.

"Tradition, colleagues, tradition," he'd begun telling them. The lawyers preened the colored feathers of their most polished dignity at this egalitarian treatment, "tradition imposes its sacred hierarchy. The top level is for the highest citizen." The Congress unanimously succumbed to the tremors of the hidden message. On the day for the award of honors they both received their decorations. "I defended you with iron and you repay me with wood," Colonel Sanabria had complained to him as the cedar cross was pinned to his uniform.

"The best gift I can give you is for you to still have some ambition left, *compadre*," he answered him softly, smiling for the photographers.

"Permission to enter, sir," an aide asked from the edge of the sunny mist that stretched out beyond the mosquito netting at the entrance. "Volunteers are coming in, sir," he explained, coming to attention and without looking directly at the army cot. "We're rounding them up with great enthusiasm, sir." The aide marched out, holding his breath.

But in the last few years the angry passion that their friendship festered in had been cooling off. They were growing old and their fear of each other was softening. Less and less frequent were the private celebrations where they raffled off women in the salon for diplomatic receptions. They were replacing sex with an appetite for power. They were growing old, and he suspected that what Sanabria most yearned for from the Greeks was more a taste of wine than the tricks of philosophy. He traveled a lot, and every time he would come back with strange ideas, weird inventions, fantasies of other worlds that couldn't possibly exist the way he told it. "If what you're telling me is true, the world is becoming liberal," Fernández told him once. "I swear to you, *compadre*," he answered. Years back it wouldn't have occurred to him to believe what he saw.

The last thing Colonel Sanabria had dropped into that little bag of mistrust of his had occurred during the revolt of the collective farmers. Out of the department of Morazan was coming news of the activities of agitators, turning people's heads, scraping away at their conformity. "Put an end to the problem," the general had concisely ordered his local commanders, but the itch went on and was spreading out like a salt stain, eating away at everything, gnawing at everything, undermining his long and laborious establishment of government. Secret agents got lost, wildly waving their arms in the web of rumors amidst the throb of the excitation that was already threatening to explode, that was growing to the very limits of fear. Mayors came and governors went; graffiti appeared on walls; soldiers' wives refused to make love on the post so as not to be caught in a bad situation at the climax; orders went out and were immediately countermanded; a flight of ominous black buzzards flew in a circle over Morazan.

That weekend Colonel Sanabria had returned hurriedly from abroad and appeared at the presidential office soon after he landed at the airport. General Fernández was standing in front of the large window in his office watching the light fall on a garden thick with gardenias and banana trees in bloom and contemplating in the distance the city orphaned by the sea. December was sewing needlework of cold onto the glass, and the north wind coming out of the mouth of the dormant volcano was beating against the window-panes. The general sensed a breath of circumspection in the room.

"What do the newspapers out there say?" he asked without turning around.

"Bad things, everything bad," the colonel answered, observing the curved back, the sagging shoulders, the protuberance around the president's waist, as if he were being embraced by a rattlesnake, a circus performer, an automobile tire. "They're calling it the barefoot revolution," he went on to explain, "and they're sure the days of your government are over."

"You mean our government," the general corrected, turning around. The glow of the sunset that reflected on the panes outlined him as a crystal giant, a huge halo of consummate will. For the first time Colonel Sanabria felt from that distance where fateful things were decided that a man more powerful than he was speaking to him—one who could decide which of its many paths death would take, one whose cruelty was unfathomable.

"So, ideas, eh, *compadre*?" the general nodded with a touch of sarcasm hanging from his lower lip, "and the papers call it the barefoot revolt, hah," he pouted with a dry rumble of determination. Colonel Sanabria had never seen him encircled by that phosphorescent halo of tranquility and wrath. This man was destiny itself, he thought.

There was a long silence, during which the president scribbled on a piece of paper with his thick desk pen, without breathing, without raising his eyes, without any sense of time.

"We're going to vaccinate the barefoot against rebellion," he finally said, calling in his secretary and giving him the handwritten telegram. "You can go in peace, *compadre*. We're going to have a peaceful Christmas," he added as he saw Sanabria out.

"What are you going to do, *compadre*?" the colonel
ventured to ask with the doorknob in his hand. He
wasn't afraid of him, he was afraid because the general
had soaked his heart with hate and it was smothering
him. The silence bounced madly about the four walls
and broke up into three little pieces of shadow.

"The people love me," the general murmured as if to
himself, standing before the window once again. "The
barefoot love me because I've given them everything," he
repeated in a monologue of conviction. "It's the edu-
cated and cultured people who are against me, the ones
who are already up in the world, the ones who can read
and learn liberal slogans. The real people love me."

Colonel Sanabria left quietly with his hat in his hand.
Outside, the secretary was waiting for him, his eyes
bulging; the colonel took the piece of paper, which was
trembling in the secretary's fingers: "Shoot everybody
with shoes on," he read. The scrawl of the general's
signature stood out like the track of a hairy spider.

It was true that everything had turned out that way,
the general reflected as he left his cot, but the stab of the
molar made him sit down again, nauseous with pain.
With his eyes half closed, he prepared a new ball of
tobacco and doubled the dose of lime, then he lay
down again and tried to doze off a little. Yes, he thought,
half asleep, that was the way it had been, but maybe he
was interpreting events too drastically. Sanabria, he
meditated, looking at the twin porcelain cups, was like
a brother, although more hesitant and cautious than
he, so much the better. Sanabria wouldn't fail him; the
general knew he wouldn't fail him even though he might
deny him and relish his own impulsive improvisations.
Besides, how many battles had there been where he
had been freed only because Sanabria had interposed
his own will of sacrifice. The three bayonet thrusts in
Acajutla had been meant for him, but Sanabria had

caught them in the soft branches of his huge lungs. Sanabria, furthermore, had requested a short song at the time of the birthday bomb. Sanabria listened to informers and made traitors confess; Sanabria deposited pocketfuls of bills to his personal account in Miami for him. Without him power would be more lonely, although less shared. His *compadre* had got deep inside of him, and the only problem was that they were after the same material things. If only he could get free of the ambition for worldly appetites, make himself immune, purified forever of human temptation, as in the splendor of Greek gods, he imagined, drifting now into a spongy whirl of drowsiness that quieted pains and memories.

An hour later a distant outbreak of shooting woke him up. "The game's starting," he said, and got up, calmer now from all his cares and pains. He arose tranquil and with a cold heart, untouched by triumph or disappointment, all the fibers of his being twisted into a skein of will. Outside there was a mixture of shouts and officers' orders giving out quick instructions for battle. He smiled when he heard neighing. Sanabria must have been returning with the powerful army that would crush the guerrillas once and for all. He walked over to the entrance of the tent and pushed the mosquito netting aside; a wave of morning smelling of sun clung to his inflamed cheek, to the white fire of his temples, his hands, circling his figure and wrapping him in luminous flashes that blinded and aged him prematurely. On the esplanade of the encampment, this side of the three reddish cannons that were now pointing at the mountains, the new soldiers were getting ready for their young battlefield apprenticeships. But the general sensed that he was a victim of the deception of sleep, an instrument of time's sleight-of-hand, a toy in the mirrors of the mind. He saw old men dragging themselves along clumsily over their oily foot rags, collapsing in the sultry stew, women raising up with forbidden efforts of the womb the heavy guns of iron and lead, children, adolescents, invalids, the sick hauling in their bungled formations the mortar caissons, shells, he caught sight of hands calloused from a hoe, sharpening lances, polishing sabers, and, for the first time, he came to know the slight mark a bare foot leaves on the dust. Behind the crowd of impressed people, aides were threatening and firing their weapons. Colonel Sanabria was riding among them, like an angel of God.

Then he discreetly called three of his veteran officers to his tent and gave his order in a cutting, unmistakable tone, like a sharp bolt of lightning: "Shoot my *compadre*," he told them. The officers were thunderstruck in the bewilderment of enigmas, impotently watching the president crossing over to the other shore of the ocean of compassion. Crushed, they went out to carry out the order.

When the thunder of the shots rang out, General Fernández stood there overwhelmed, looking at the translucent walls of his quarters. "*Compadre*," he lamented wearily, as if conversing with a dead man, "we believe what we want to believe, but reality imposes itself." He began to shuffle through the piles of regulations and the notebooks with decrees for the rules governing posthumous decorations for heroes who had fallen in battle under the sun's harsh clutch.

Translated by Gregory Rabassa

The Perfect Game

Sergio Ramírez

 Usually as he rushed out of the tunnel into the stands, his eyes went straight to the bullpen to see if the kid was warming up. Had the manager finally decided to use him as starter? Tonight, though, his bus had broken down on the South Highway, and he had arrived so late that the Boer-San Fernando game was already well under way. Back in the urine-smelling tunnel he'd heard the umpire's screech of "Strike!"; so now, with dinner pail under one arm and bottle under the other, he hurried out into the dazzling whiteness, which seemed to float down like a milky haze from the depths of the starry sky.

He always tried to get to the stadium before the San Fernando manager had handed his team's lineup to the head umpire, while the pitchers were still warming up in the bullpen. Sometimes his son would be one of them, so he would press up against the wire fence, his fingers gripping the wire, to show him he was there, that he had arrived. The boy was too shy to acknowledge his presence and invariably kept on practising in that silent, ungainly way of his. But by the beginning of the game he had always been back on the bench: never once since San Fernando had signed him for the big league at the opening of the season had he started as pitcher. Some nights he hadn't even warmed up, and he would shake his head at his father from the shadows of the dugout: No, it wasn't going to be tonight either.

And now, just when he had got there so late, he scanned the green of the floodlit field and spotted him at once on the pitcher's mound. There he was, a thin, slightly hunched figure, following the catcher's signals intently. Before his father could put the dinner pail down to adjust his glasses, he saw him wind up and pitch.

"Strike!" he heard the umpire shout a second time in the sweltering night. He peered down again, shielding his eyes with his hand: it was him, his boy was pitching, they'd put him on to start. He saw him casually field the ball the catcher returned to him, then wipe the sweat from his brow with the glove. He still needs a bit of polish, he's still raw, his father thought proudly.

He picked up the dinner pail and, as if frightened of making any noise, walked carefully, almost on tiptoe, to the limit of the cheap seats behind home plate, as close as he could get to the San Fernando dugout. He had no idea of how the game stood. He was aware only that at last his boy was up there on the mound under the floodlights, while out beyond the scoreboard and the stands stretched the vast black night.

He paused as a harmless infield fly floated up. The shortstop took a few steps back and spread his arms wide to show it was his catch. He caught it safely, threw the ball back to the mound, then the whole team trotted off to the dugout. End of inning. His boy strolled off, staring at his feet.

The stadium was almost empty. There was no applause or shouting, the atmosphere was more like a practice match when a few curious onlookers drift into the stadium and huddle together in tiny groups, as if to keep warm.

Still standing, he looked over at the scoreboard above the brightly colored billboards, high in the stadium beyond the direct light of the floodlights and already half in shadow. The scoreboard itself was like a housefront with windows. The men who hung the figures in the two windows that showed the score for each inning were silhouetted against it. One of these shadows was busy closing the window for the bottom of the fourth inning with a nought.

	1	2	3	4	5	6	7	8	9		H	E
SAN FERNANDO	0	0	0	0							0	0
BOER	0	0	0	0							0	0

Boer hadn't managed to hit against his boy, and his team had made no errors, so he was pitching a perfect game. A perfect game—as he cleaned his glasses, breathing on them then wiping them on his shirt, with the bottle still tucked under one arm and the dinner pail on the floor beside him.

He walked up a few steps to be with the nearest group of spectators. He sat next to a fat man with a blotchy white face who sold lottery tickets. He was surrounded by a halo of peanut shells. He split the shells with his teeth, spat them out, then chewed on the nuts. The father carefully set the dinner pail and the bottle down. He had brought the dinner his wife always prepared for the boy to eat after the game. The bottle was full of milky coffee.

91

"No runs at all?" he looked back awkwardly to ask the others, to make sure the scoreboard was correct. A stiff neck he'd had for years made it hard for him to turn his head. The fat man looked at him with the easy familiarity of baseball fans. Everybody in the stands knows one another, even if they've never met before.

"Runs?" he exclaimed, as though taken aback by a blasphemy, but still chewing steadily. "They haven't even got to first base with that skinny kid pitching for San Fernando."

"He's only a boy," a woman in the row behind said, pursing her lips in pity as if he really were still a small child. She had gold teeth and wore pebble glasses. Between her feet was a large handbag, at which she kept glancing down anxiously.

Another of the spectators sitting higher up chuckled a toothless grin, "Where the hell did they dig up such a beanpole?" The father struggled to turn his head properly so he could see who was insulting his boy. He fiddled with his glasses to get a clearer view of him and to glare his reproach. One of the sidepieces of his glasses was missing, so he had them tied around one ear with a shoelace.

"He's my son," he announced to the whole group, staring at them defiantly despite the crick in his neck. The gap-toothed heckler still had a sarcastic smile on his face, but didn't say a word. Still spitting out shells, the fat man patted his leg. No runs, no hits, no errors? His son was out there, pitching for the first time, and he had a clean sheet. He felt at home in the stands.

And now he heard on the rumbling loudspeakers that it was his boy who was going to open the inning for San Fernando. He didn't last long. One of the assistants threw a jacket around his shoulders to keep his arm warm.

"He's no great shakes as a batter," his father explained, to no one in particular.

"There's no such thing as a pitcher who can bat," the woman answered. It was strange to see her without her husband, alone in this group of men. She ought to be at home in bed at that time of night, he thought; but she knows a thing or two about the game. His own wife had never wanted to go with him to the stadium at night. She prepared the boy's food, then sat in the room that served as shoe repair shop, kitchen and dining room, glued to the radio, though she couldn't really follow the action.

The San Fernando team was taking to the field again after getting nothing from their half-inning. His boy was strolling back to the mound. Bottom of the fifth inning.

"Let's see how he does," the fat man grunted affectionately. "I've been a Boer fan all my life, but I take my hat off to a good pitcher." With that, he swept off his yellow cap with its Allis-Chalmer badge in salute.

Boer's fourth batter was the first at the plate. He was a Yankee import and was chewing gum or tobacco. To judge by the bulging cheek and the way he spat constantly, it must have been tobacco. All his boy needed were three pitches. Three marvellous strikes—the last of them a curve that broke beautifully over the outer edge of the plate. The Yank never even touched it. He looked stunned.

"He didn't see them," the woman laughed. "That kid's growing up fast."

Then there was an easy grounder to the shortstop. The last batter popped out to the third baseman. All three were out in no time.

"Will you look at that," gap-tooth shouted. "That beanpole's no pushover." Too bad there were so few people to hear him. The stands all around them were empty, and he could see only a few cigarette butts glowing down in the reserved seats section under the lights from the radio commentators' boxes. This time he didn't even bother to turn around to the smart-ass. Fifteen outs in a row. Would his wife be beside the radio back home? She must have understood some of it, if only the name of her boy.

The San Fernando team was batting again. The top of the sixth inning. One of them got to first with a quick bunt, then the catcher, number five in their line-up, hit a double, and the man on first made a desperate run of the bases and just scraped home. That was all: the top of the sixth was over—with one run on the scoreboard.

"Well," the fat Boer supporter said sadly, "now your boy is one up."

That was the first time he'd called him "your boy". And there he was, strolling out, hunched and frail, back to the mound, his features lengthened under the shadow of his cap. Just a kid, as the woman had said.

"He'll be eighteen in June," he confided to his neighbor, but the fat man was suddenly on his feet cheering, because the ball was flying off the bat out to centerfield. His own heart leapt as he saw the ball soaring into the outfield, but over by the billboards, where the lettering glistened as though it had just rained, the center-fielder was running back to make the catch. He collided noisily with the fence, but held the ball. Disappointed, the fat man sat down again. "Good hit," was all he said.

Next there was a grounder behind third base. The third baseman scooped it up behind the bag and threw it as hard as he could. Out at first.

"The team's doing all it can for your boy," the woman said.

"Whose side are you on now, Doña Teresa?" the fat man asked, annoyed.

94

"I never take sides. I only come to bet, but today there's nothing going," she replied, unruffled. Her bag was full of money to bet on anything: ball or strike, base hit or error, run or not. And the fat man came to sell his lottery tickets in those little packets.

The third man hit a chopper right in front of the plate. The catcher grabbed it and threw to first. The batter didn't even bother to run. This incensed the fat man.

"What are they paying that chicken for? . . . Up yours!" he bawled through cupped hands.

Someone strolled down from the deserted stands, a small blue plastic transistor pressed to his ear. The fat man called to him by name, "What does Sucre make of this?"

"He says there's the chance of a perfect game," the man replied, imitating the voice of the famous commentator, Sucre Frech.

"Is that what he says?" the father gasped, his voice thick with emotion. He fiddled with the loop of the shoelace behind his ear, as though that would help him hear better.

"Turn your radio up," the fat man demanded. The other put it down on the ground and turned it louder. The fat man lifted his hand in an automatic gesture of throwing a peanut into his mouth, then began to chew . . . "All of you who couldn't be bothered to turn up tonight are missing out on something really fantastic: the first chance in the history of the country to see a perfect game. You've no idea what you're missing."

It was the top of the seventh: the fateful inning. San Fernando was batting. The first man walked, but then was picked off trying to steal. The second hit the ball straight back at the pitcher. The third was struck out. The game was fast and furious.

Now it was Boer's turn to bat in the lucky seventh. His boy would have to take on the big guns, who were bound to make him squirm. The seventh inning: the one for the stretch, for surprises and scares. Everyone sweating with anticipation.

He was trembling, in the grip of a fever despite the heat. He looked back painfully to see the gap-tooth's expression, but the man was sitting silently and seemed miles away, all his attention turned to the radio. Sucre Frech's voice was lost in a crackle of static on the warm breeze.

The umpire's shout was real, tangible. "Strike three!" His boy had struck out the first batter.

"That beanpole is hurling rocks out there," the man behind muttered, his chin cupped in his hands as though he were praying.

He caught sight of the ball floating gently up into the white light. The left fielder raced down the line to get under it . . . got into position . . . waited . . . caught the ball! The second out. The woman slapped her knees excitedly. "That's the way, that's the way!" The stands appeared back-to-front in the thick pebbles of her glasses. The fat man kept on chewing air without a word.

The first ball was too high. The gap-tooth stood up as though to stretch his legs, but nobody was fooled. A foul off to the back. Strike one.

That made it one and one. Another foul. One and two. The field stretched out, calm and peaceful. The out-fielders stood motionless halfway back to the fence. A truck rumbled in the distance along the South Highway.

Another foul to the back—three in a row. The batter wouldn't give up. "Strike!" The ball sped right down the middle. The batter didn't even have time to react and stood there with his bat still aloft. End of the seventh inning!

A ripple of applause, like the rustle of dry leaves. The clapping drifted slowly up to him in the deserted stand. He laughed out loud, knowing that all of them in the group around him, even gap-tooth and the fat man, were as pleased as he was.

"This is a great moment," the fat man declared. "I wouldn't have missed this for anything, even though it hurts."

Sucre Frech was talking about Don Larsen, who in a World Series only two years previously had pitched the *only* perfect game in the *history* of the major leagues . . . "and now it looks as if this unknown Nicaraguan pitcher is about to achieve the same feat, step by step, pitch by pitch."

They were talking in the same breath of Don Larsen and his boy, who at that moment was walking back to the dugout, where he sat calmly at the far end, like it was nothing. His teammates were chatting, again like it was nothing. Their manager looked unconcerned. Managua was slumbering in the dark, like it was nothing. And he too was sitting there as if nothing had happened—he hadn't even gone down to the fence, as he usually did, to let the kid know he was there.

"An obscure rookie who I'm told is from Masatepe, signed only this season by San Fernando. This is his first time to start as a pro, his first chance, and here he is pitching a perfect game. Who could believe it?"

"A perfect game means glory," the fat man concurred, listening devotedly to the radio.

"It's straight to the major leagues, first thing tomorrow. And you can scoop the jackpot," the woman cackled, rubbing her fingers together. The father felt keyed up, floating on air. He gave a mocking sideways glance at his tormentor, as though to say: "What d'you make of your beanpole now?" but the gap-toothed man simply nodded his head without demur.

The loudspeakers repeated the name of San Fernando's first batter. He reached first base with an infield hit. The second man hit into a double play to the shortstop. The last batter was struck out, and the inning was over.

"Get a move on, I want to see the beanpole pitch!" gap-tooth shouted as Boer trooped off the field, but nobody found it funny. "Sshh!" the fat man silenced him.

Once again all the lights for strikes and outs disappeared from the distant scoreboard. Now for the bottom of the eighth. Everybody hold on to your hats!

His boy was back on the mound. Sweat was coursing down his face as he again studied the catcher's signals. What he'd done that night was real enough, he was making history with his arm. Did they know in Masatepe? Would the people on his block have stayed up to listen? Surely they must have heard the news. They'd have flung open their doors, switched on all the lights, gathered on street corners, to hear how a local boy was pitching a perfect game.

Strike one! Straight past the batter.

It was the Yank's turn again. He punched the air with the bat, the wad of tobacco bulging in his cheek. Before he even realized, the kid had sent a second strike past him. He never pitched a bad one, every single pitch was on target. Another lightning throw: Strike three, and out! The Yank flung down the bat so furiously it nearly bounced into the Boer dugout. The gap-toothed fan jeered him.

"Know something?" the fat man with the lottery tickets nudged the old man. "Another five outs and you'll join the ranks of the immortals too, because you're his father."

Sucre Frech was talking about immortality at that very moment on the little blue radio rattling on the cement steps. About the immortals of this sport of kings. The whole of Managua ought to be there to witness the entry of a humble, obscure young man into immortality. He nodded, chill with fear, yes, the whole of Managua should have been there, hurrying out of the tunnels, filling all the seats, dressed in pyjamas, slippers, nightshirts. They should be leaping out of bed, hailing taxis or scurrying on foot to see this great feat, this unrepeatable marvel . . . a line drive cutting between center and left field . . . the fielder appeared out of nowhere, running forward with his arm outstretched to stop the ball as if by magic; then he coolly threw it back. The second out of the inning!

He wanted to get to his feet, but his courage failed him. The woman had covered her face in her hands, and was peering through spread fingers. The toothless wonder tapped him on the shoulder.

"They want to interview you on Radio Mundial when this inning is over. Sucre Frech in person," he said, whistling tunelessly through the gap in his teeth.

"How do they know he's the boy's father?" the fat man enquired.

"I told them," grinned the other man smugly . . . a low ball near first base, the first baseman stopped it, the pitcher assisted, another easy out! End of inning!

"We'll all go," the fat man said imperiously.

They stood up. The fat man led the way up to the Radio Mundial commentary box. When they got there, high up beyond the empty rows of seats, Sucre Frech passed the microphone out his window. The father grasped it fearfully. Gap-tooth pushed in next to him. The woman, her handbag full of money clamped firmly on her arm, stood there grinning, showing off all her gold teeth as if she were having her portrait taken by a photographer. The fat man cocked his head to listen.

"You tell 'em, old fella," he encouraged the father.

He can't remember what he said, apart from sending greetings to all the fans everywhere in Nicaragua, and especially those in Masatepe, to his wife, the pitcher's mother, and to everyone in *barrio* Veracruz.

He would have liked to add: It was me who made a pitcher of him, I've been training that arm since he was thirteen; at fifteen he started for the General Moncada team for the first time; I used to take him on the back of my bike every day to practice; I sewed his first glove in my shoe shop; it was me who made those spikes he's wearing.

But he had no time for any of that. Sucre Frech snatched the microphone back to begin his commentary on San Fernando's ninth and final inning. They were still in the lead, one to nothing. Just think what all of you who stayed at home are missing.

Again San Fernando failed to add to their score. By the time the group was back in its place in the stand, one of the batters had been struck out and the others followed in rapid succession. Now came the moment of truth everyone had been waiting for. Boer's last chance, the final challenge for the boy whose stature had grown so immensely as the evening wore on:

	1	2	3	4	5	6	7	8	9
SAN FERNANDO	0	0	0	0	1	0	0	0	0
BOER	0	0	0	0	0	0	0	0	

All that was needed was one last circle on the board, to close the last window where in the distance the score keeper's head was visible. They wouldn't even trouble to put up the final score; they never did at the end of the game.

There was a respectful silence as his boy sauntered out to the center of the diamond, as though he were leaving for a long journey. From high in the stands, his

100

father saw him shoot a glance in his direction, to reassure himself that he was there, that he hadn't failed to come on this of all nights. Should I have gone down there? he reproached himself.

"I'm right not to have gone down there, aren't I?" he asked his neighbor in a low voice.

"Sure," the fat man gave his judgement, "when his perfect game is over, we'll all go down and congratulate him."

Ball—too high, the first pitch. The catcher had to go on tiptoe to take it. Bottom of the ninth inning: one ball, no strikes.

"I can't bear to look," the woman said, ducking behind her handbag.

Up at bat was a black Cuban from the Sugar Kings. The kid had already struck him out once. He stood there, wiry and muscular in his freshly laundered uniform, impatiently tapping his heels with the bat.

"That black's out to bust the stitching off the ball," gap-tooth pronounced.

The second pitch was too high as well. With no sign of emotion, the umpire turned aside to note down another ball. Two balls, no strikes.

"This is a fine time to crack up, kid," the gap-tooth man muttered, speaking for all the group.

The third pitch is also a ball, Sucre Frech screamed into the microphone.

"What's going on?" the woman asked from behind her bag.

"What a crying shame," the fat man commiserated, looking at him with genuine pity. But all he was aware of was the sweat soaking his hatband.

The catcher called time-out and trotted over to the mound to talk to the boy. He listened hard, slapping the ball into his glove the whole while.

The discussion on the mound was over. The catcher slipped his mask back on, and the batter returned to the plate. If the next throw was a ball, the black man in the starched white uniform could throw down the bat mockingly and stroll to first base, jubilant at someone else's misfortune.

"Strike!" shouted the umpire in the hushed silence, flailing his arm in the air. As his cry died away, it was so quiet they could almost hear the lights hissing on top of their towers.

"Bound to happen," said the gap-toothed Boer fan.

Now the score stood at three balls, one strike. No outs. Sucre Frech was silent too. A buzz of static was the only sound from the radio.

The father sat bent over, hugging his knees, but still feeling exposed, unprotected. In his mind though he was sailing off into the same milky vapor that drifted down from the floodlights, from the sky full of stars. He floated painfully away.

"Strike!" the umpire's voice rang out again.

"The whole of Managua heard that one," the fat man chortled.

The Cuban had flung himself at the ball with all his might. He spun around, and stood teetering, trying to regain his balance.

"If he does connect, we'll never see the ball again," the toothless tormentor said, still preaching in the wilderness.

Three balls, two strikes. Anyone with heart problems had better switch off their radio now and read what happened in tomorrow's papers.

His boy caught a new ball. He studied it quizzically. Still cowering behind her handbag, the woman wanted to know what was happening now. "Shut up!" the fat man snapped.

The black man blasted a high fly, which the wind carried over to the San Fernando dugout, close by where they were sitting. The catcher chased it desperately, but in the end the ball bounced harmlessly on the roof of the covered seats.

"That leaves the count at three and two," gap-tooth mimicked the radio.

"Are you trying to be funny?" the fat man had his blood up . . . a grounder between shortstop and third, the shortstop chased it, picked it up, threw to first base. Out!

All his hope flooded to his throat, then burst out in a triumphant shout that washed all over them. Would his boy come straight back with him to Masatepe? Fireworks, everybody in the streets: he'd have to lock up, he didn't want everything stolen.

The red eye on the scoreboard showed the first out.

"Nearly there, nearly there," crooned the woman.

The fat man put an arm around his shoulder, and the gap-toothed man was cheekily patting him on the back. The owner of the radio had turned it up full volume to celebrate.

"Don't congratulate me yet," he begged them, shrugging them off. But what he really felt like saying was yes, congratulate me, hug me all of you, let's laugh and enjoy ourselves.

The sudden crack of the bat made them all swivel their gaze back to the field. The white shape of the ball stood out sharply as it bounced near second base. The fielder was waiting for it behind the bag. He ran to one side, stopped, picked it up, pulled it from his glove to throw to first. He fumbled it, juggled with the ball for what seemed an eternity, finally held it, threw . . . threw wide!

The batter sped past first base. The father turned to the others. He still had a smile on his face, but now he was imploring them to confirm that this was crazy, that it hadn't happened. Yet there was the first base umpire in black, bent almost double, his arms sweeping the ground, while the batter stood his ground defiantly and tossed his protective helmet away.

The radio owner turned the sound down, so they could no longer make out what Sucre Frech was saying up in the box.

"After the error comes the hit," the gap-toothed man prophesied pitilessly.

The few photographers at the game gathered around home plate.

Another clear thud from the bat pulled him out of himself as out of a lonely miserable well.

The ball bounced far out into centerfield and hit the fence. The runner on first easily reached third; the throw was aimed at the catcher to stop him there, but it sailed yards wide, and almost hit the dugout. The flashbulbs told them the tying run had been scored.

The second batter was rounding third base, the ball was still loose; the second man slid home in a cloud of dust, the cameras flashed again.

"Boer has done it, you jerks!" the fat man chortled. Crestfallen, the father blinked at his companions. "What now?" he asked in a feeble voice.

"That's the way it goes," the gap-toothed man behind him said, already standing up to leave.

The small crowd was hurrying out the gates, all the excitement forgotten. The fat man smoothed his trousers down, feeling for change in his pocket. San Fernando had already left the field. The fat man and the woman trundled off, deep in conversation.

The father picked up the dinner pail and the bottle of by-now-cold coffee. He pushed open the wire gate and walked out onto the field. Swallowed up in the darkness of the dugout, the players were busy changing to go home. He sat on the bench next to his boy and untied the cloth around the dinner pail. His uniform soaked in sweat, his spikes caked with dirt, the boy began silently to eat. With every mouthful, he looked over at his father. He chewed, took a drink from the bottle, looked at him.

The boy took off his cap for the sweat in his hair to dry. A sudden gust of wind swept a cloud of dust from the diamond and plucked the cap from the bench. His father jumped up and ran after it, finally catching up with it beyond home plate.

From right field they began to put out the lights. Only the two of them were left in the stadium, surrounded by the silent stands that the night was reclaiming.

He walked back with the cap and replaced it gently on his son's head. The boy kept on eating.

Translated by Nick Caistor

In the Shade of a Little Old Lady in Flower

Alfonso Quijada Urías

A demented sun twisting like a snake in the orphaned, turbulent landscape. Each day's noisy confusion, the city under siege. Thousands of building eyes pondering: How long? The mute history of organized everydayness. State of siege. Demented states. Sirens of Ulysses, driver for the fire department. People walking fast, complaining about the heat and the crush in the sardine can buses. Deadly feelings of dread. Fear of dying while walking along these San Sivar Streets, these España and Delano Roosevelt Avenues. Dead air that I breathe as I live. Bullets whistle. Cannons bleat. The demented sun fires a sweaty heat. Brash. The radio in the Flower of Paris Shoestore at full blast: the national anthem as main course. A gloomy voice from the bottom of a well announcing the state of siege. All days meet their end on the tin roofs, cultivated by the sun. Flowering coins covering the city. Clouds on the horizon. Flocks of black sheep on the steep slope, bleating. Weeping mourners.

That's how things are here. Behind that apparent calm in the cafeterias, behind that fake calm a whirlwind—turmoil. And suddenly the cars spin around. They come back in the opposite direction. Crash. Twist around each other. Nobody pays attention to traffic lights. Shots. Gunfire. Flight of frightened pigeons. Terrified. "It's on San Miguelito," shouts the real estate salesman. "They went into the bank." All four dead. ("Terrorists" the *Daily Devil* will say. On page one.) Later it was learned that one of them was a pastor of the Latter Day Saints. Another was found with a "Don Quixote" notebook containing love poems. Celia heard the same story. The cab driver told her all the gory details. He was cornered, sweating like a pig on a corner of San Miguelito. That's how they tell the thousand and one stories about that infernal day.

That same afternoon. At the age of one hundred, moving straight from eternity to eternity, the mother of invention died. She died. What a bright idea at her age, to die pre-cise-ly during these days. Black days.

She died because she felt like it, because she no longer liked this world. This infernal world. Sordid. She was the grandma of the neighborhood. Of the district. Of life. Was there anyone who didn't know her? She fought the pimps with her stiletto. She got drunk on weekends and holidays. A voracious reader of Eugene Sue, Vargas Vila, and Genoveva de Brabante. She played card games and Chinese checkers with astounding skill. There were times when she got itchy feet or was plagued by unshakeable, obsessive ideas and would travel by mule to the mountains of Honduras. She would go off with her ornate boxes, porcelain treasures, magnet stones, laces, patent leather slippers, gold coins, silkalines, needles, enchanted birds, song books, magic powders, devotionals—and so many other things that had their proper place in a complete inventory.

That day (all days meet their end) her funeral service was held. Decent just as she dreamed it would be. Everybody was there, congregated. Legendary family legions. Generations of generations. Origin of her species. Incredibly distant relatives. So distant they seemed invisible, unnameable. That entire universe spoke about her: Great saintly woman. Without a navel. Without sin. Pure as a white parchment womb. Cauliflower vagina.

What was the matter? Where was the problem? Without a birth certificate there is no death certificate, to certify the journey. The document of her birth had been lost. Seed of her origin.

Afterward Adam told the story of that mess. We had to consult dignitaries, magistrates, ailing old men. Create a great flight of pigeons. Knock on thousands of doors, walk across salons, impenetrable houses. Patios filled with brilliant flowers and leaves. We sat with the doctors of the law, interrogated the greatest great-grandfather of them all. It took us forever to find out. To discover the original version. The grand old man solved it at last. Her name was Cleotilde Barrios. Not Isadora Cartagena as she called herself. She was born on a Thursday, the third of March 1899, in La Vega District. "Said information attested to by the father of the child in the presence of the Municipal Secretary." Whose signature was affixed to the present document.

After all that trouble came the burial, which was even more complicated because of having to cross the city in wartime. We had to take the risk. Of course. Tides of war broke against the wall of the Sisters of Charity. The quiet trees, the green leaves of translucent jade. His eye is on the sparrow. We had to give her a holy burial. Take the risk of the difficult pilgrimage. Go up Arce. Cross España. Turn on to Dario. Come out on El Calvario and then straight ahead on Cementerio General. And bury her at last. Yes. With all due speed. Give her a holy burial in this time of war. Apocalyptic sorrow. Trumpets of Jericho. Wailing Wall. Mother of mine.

And there we go. Behind the hearse, black, solemn. How serious they are, the dead and those who bury them. The ones in the funeral procession. The little man with his black suit and his account book. The driver and his Charlie Chaplin moustache. And those peculiar odors: a mortal breath, lilies, cologne, chemical decomposition of the body, wreaths of flowers. Between the scent of life and of death. And us— remembering, ceremoniously thoughtful, those days of our great mother. Remembering the times when she drank her "cane spirits." Her elixir of life. And sang and cursed half the world. She advised her daughters to forget all that crap about virginity. Gave advice about everything. At night she recounted her old adventures. Her stories about when she enlisted as purveyor of provisions in the armed forces of General Mendieta, in '26. Or else her countless love affairs. We went back to the pure fountain. To the original patio. To the cosmic return of the great mother. And we saw her as she was on that day of her return from the war in Honduras with her spoils of war—two trucks full of liquor, four juke boxes, three freezers, two bars, five sets of living-room furniture, six dining rooms, two pool tables, and more junk than could fit into an account book. All of us. That beautiful day we went out to meet her, moved, patriotic. That was a fiesta without end. Six weeks when the tremendous din of the music did not stop. Night and day. Day and night.

"Listen," I said to the driver, "try not to go through the center of town. There's always trouble around the post office." But he thought he knew it all, and his only answer was to wiggle his tiny Charlie Chaplin moustache. "Look," I insisted again, "it's better to avoid any problems. It's better for you to take the side streets going toward Plazuela Barrios or Policía Street." But the man continued straight ahead with his wooden face. Expressionless. His nothing's-going-on-here face.

And so we moved at a snail's pace, through that peaceful central district, following the black car; having premonitions of disaster. We passed along Arce: the little square of San José. Second-hand book stalls. Shoeshine boys. Pigeons. Flocks of pigeons cleaning the dirty hot four o'clock air with their whiteness. Water ice and ice cream stands. Schoolgirls, blue and white, faces painted in the style of the latest *Vanidades*. Tigresses and vampires. Just ordinary people. The lady with elephantiasis at the foot of the General Electric building. And further on, drunkards and tourists coming out of Chico's Bar and the New World Hotel. Old bars filled with old binges.

There. Right then. That's when the trouble began. Like the roar of the sea. People scattering. Then the sound of sirens and gunfire, and the cars began to spin around, to lose their sense of direction. Crashing. Motors turning off. Accelerating, bellowing, doors slamming. That's how the trouble began. After the gunfire came the panic. Everybody running, jumping, looking for a way out. A safe place just as the heavy grates of the bakeries, the shops, the cafeterias came slamming

111

down. Because after fire and disaster come the devouring locusts. Looting—base, shameless. "Another student massacre. The ones who occupied the cathedral," shouted a woman in terror. "Monsignor just came out." Everything is red. Red-hot. Sunsets and roses. Blood of our blood. The massacred will be avenged. Río Lempa 1930 and twice as bloody. Steps covered with blood, skin, brains. Another funeral pyre.

In the distance, scattered spots. Multitudes like heads of pins. Dots running in every direction, through the smoke and ashen explosions of the afternoon. A bus enveloped in flames on the corner of Dragón.

Through great vicissitudes, with the ancient and astute instinctive logic of the fox, we escaped from danger. From the labyrinth, the disastrous confusion, the hecatomb. Far from the fire zone. Making our way, retreating, advancing. We plunged into alleys, ancient passageways, ruined mansions, old places in a San Salvador that was anonymous, primitive. Remains of railroads, wagons. Way stations for mules. Old and solemn barbershops like The Little French Girl and Figaro. Yes, escaping by twists and turns. Finally we reach the cemetery. Scattered. Terrified. Coming to the main gate from different directions. All of us. Except the hearse. Except the remains of one who had once been. Just one of those things.

There we are. Nervous. Cigarette after cigarette of not finding the thread of the matter. Ariadne's thread. Whacanyado? We waited for things to settle down so we could look for the coffin. Lost ark. Urn of our empress.

Other stories began to surface. No less bizarre. Could the hearse have been run down by the immense sardine can bus? Or did they pick up the driver as a suspect? With the car and all? Opinions surfaced. The most desperate: We would have to call the Red Cross or the Fire Department. Another one. Pay for an announcement on Radio KL asking for information regarding the whereabouts of a solemn funeral hearse—'66 Chevrolet, four door, license number 26000. Bearing the mortal remains of Cleotilde Barrios, known far and wide as The Bandit.

But it was all in vain. Vanity of vanities. While we thought and thought again the shadows were falling. Chinese. Ink blots on the white mausoleums, on the graves, on the dark earth. And as they closed the gate, creaking of plaintive doors, the hearse turned the corner. Twice as black. Sepulchral. And then came a terrible absurd joy with shouts of *hurrah* and *Viva!* Stony astonishment afterward. Black spring.

We were in a rush to bury her. To leave her once and for all in the peace or war of her holy sepulcher. Then came the tears, seas of weeping, gnashing of teeth, sighs, fainting, hearts pounding. We had to pay the funereal little man. The custodian who refused to open—regulations in hand—the portentous portals. We cursed frantically at the stubborn driver and were ready to lynch him for having put us through moments of such crisis. And so. At last. He gave in to our pleas. The skinny little man opened the great gate again.

Leaping. Almost falling flat on our faces over tombstones and mausoleums we finally came to her grave. Empty as a round *O*. As the mouth of nothingness. Mouthful of smoke. Lowering the varnished mortuary ark with straps, coffer of what once was, to the bottom of the earth. Wood creaking. We left them. Her remains. Ready. Deposited in the dark kingdom of eternity. Then came the earth. Spongy—falling hard and heavy, loose and dark over the glass and wood. Producing a muffled noise, of drums. The lugubrious drum that bids farewell to the dead. The tom-tom of death.

And again, of course, seas of weeping, hurricanes of sighs, jungles of shouts and laments.

At last. All days meet their end. The funereal urn lost in its funeral kingdom. Sealed under a thousand and one blankets of earth, very deep. Packed down by earth: hard, compact, black and loose. We were in a great rush to bury her. A great rush before the night grew any deeper.

When we reached home our mother was there. Behind the curtain. In her wicker rocking chair, with a glass of "spirits" in her hand. Rocking. As if nothing at all had happened. Nothing at all.

Translated by Edith Grossman

Tarantulas of Honey

Pedro Rivera

I

Of course, her work. What can I say? It's a living . . . a life preserved in time, mimetic among faces and immersions. Under the eyelids of the night, structurally absorbed; in sequence, connected. Understanding this has its problems. It's a Pandora's box. Not because I am really ignorant and afraid (perhaps afraid). In my case, living within fixed norms and breaking them has its charms, even though going beyond them leaves a taste of dirt in the mouth. Sounds, tension and harsh dissonance, lights turning like tortoise fins, colors of drained neon penetrate, scratch at my memory. Alcohol doesn't work. I drink just for fun, almost in order not to drink. And I look at her, scrutinize her. She cuts through angles, exhausts the structures of the dance under the reflector lights, spreads open with impunity like a chaste appendage. I play the fool, of course, looking at her like

115

this, through the phosphorescent smoke. It feels as if a tiger claw were piercing my chest, dancing there. I look under the table. I want to know if I'm wearing socks, if one is red and the other blue, if people have realized it and pretend they're not looking at me. I try to do what everybody else does, get into the show, keep time, applaud on cue—in brief, a catastrophe.

I do not explore; I am simply there, forced to a stop by a flat tire. As simple as that—a kind of silent pleasure in loosening the bolts, lifting several tons with the turn of a lever, hydraulic jack, point of contact, metaphysics of balance. And then, then to pull away at full speed, smell the burning oil, the stench of the exhaust.

Ana on stage, in apotheosis, Anita in the light—exposed, submerged in spasms of choreography, and her index finger, a pelican beak, an asp violating, wounding the audience (underground idea), biting the folds of expectation. Delirium that never reaches tremens, an irritant, an attempt to climb deserted roofs, thread a needle in the dark. Art? Cornucopia in ruins? A woman with volatile buttocks, before, before and after Anita, spits her belly out of her mouth, whirls her breastbone on a pubic axis, presses her body with the tips of her fingers, supple. "What can you do?" I say.

She interprets ballads in Mona Bell time, cute as a dusky little monkey bell. After the song she comes to the table. My hands, greasy (it's fear, I swear it), touch her soft down, her tanned otter skin. I look at her with the eyes of a mountain climber; I undress her even more than she is already undressed; I climb up her silence; I am a cat. Rosa came over with her, sits down, gulps her drink quickly, puts in her two cents worth of stupid chatter, worse jokes. I explain the difference between free-swimming fish and food fish, how one becomes the other. The fish caught in the net can fight, flip over, try to slip through a tear in the net. In the end it's decided: sizzle at the bottom of a frying pan.

It goes on, talk talk talk. I am you are he is. The moods and tenses of the verb, the nominative adjectives, vice versa. Talk talk talk, each word clothed with a little fire worthy of higher things, the empyrean, proving that, a little to the left, one is different because of a university education and all the rest of it. I recognize the incongruity of my Don Juanism. I try to go with the flow, a little to the right I am a stranger, ready to use my strangeness as a resource, a tactic. I can simplify the entire process, slap a nice new twenty against her thighs, push the accelerator to the floor, press buttons, look for the crack in the door where I can slip in three dollars—oh, Anita, roof, flat tire, and be consumed in her, be humiliated. It's the way to end it once and for all. Afterwards she won't charge anything to say good-bye; she will know what to do after the spasms, with that Amazonian humility traced under her arched eyelashes, she will whisper in my ear that she had a wonderful time. She'll say I'm a stallion.

I am looking for another way, communication on another plane, intellectual anguish, to see if I can do it. And so I talk about her country (later I will realize that she has no country). I shake loose old memories, I dust off streets that lead nowhere, plazas, pine woods at the crossroads of heaven, mute adolescence. She is bored. San Cristobal Santa Lucia Gran Bretaña Mapocho Las Condes, cinematographic flights, places in ruins, nothing. I know Santiago, I tell her—book fairs, political demonstrations, The Bim Bam Bum. The picaresque Pollo Dorado, *boîtes* buried in basements, child singers, muggers, rickety jitneys, tarts, shabby hotels, shanty towns, all of that, my remembrances: she doesn't give a damn, to her they're worn-out old shoes, trash. Her

117

mother has cancer, she tells me. She has two children (triple-cancer). With academic indulgence I don't ask their ages, their sex means nothing to me. I go in at her level; I don't care if she loves them or if they are a burden. I respect her silence. I don't bring up subjects that will make the whiskey bitter, use up the cigarettes, or shatter the magic, the alchemy of the moment.

The whiskey gallops across whole territories of silence, emptiness, alternatives. I can't escape, my hands are tied, the night has no exit. The guitars turning up the amp; the drums, the organ weighed down with years (the old man who plays it is vitaminized in the rhythm) come down with us to the nocturnal, artificial steppe. Crowded into the prism of flashing light, to compensate for interstellar, concrete lack of communication, where glass chair trumpet cage doremifasolati champagne bikini ashtray lights men's room ladies' room microphones loudspeakers I she trace out relationships, single superimposed destinies. She moves away, returns to her number on the stage, the previous voluptuous hip abandons the platform; Ana's song now introduces successive planes in diversity. I perceive a longing to give herself to the song, a frustrated plenitude under the crude surface of minimal clothing, agitated breasts, dry breathing.

II

Enrique, I know him. I look at his pale, provocative tribal face. Ana is not there; she's been gone a week for no apparent reason. Rosa is working two bureaucrats, accumulating chips; those groping caresses under the table, that stroking of thighs, it's costing them a lot. She's introduced me to Nicho, her lover; she leaves him at my table so she can have her hands free.

"Suck up your drink, Julio," Nicho tells me.

His talk is like the steady flow of a sewage pipe. He is surprised at my sobriety. He is the center. He talks about himself, he loves himself; everything that is not him is something that he deduces from his own point of view: "The new girls are all rotten," he says.

"See her, Rita?" he points with his finger. "She did her number with me, not bad, know what I mean?"

"Which one?" I ask.

"That clumsy-looking broad," he says. "She's after me for more. She can still taste it. I did a good job on her, ya' know?"

Enrique presses my hand, does it so I can see his left hand feeling under the garish clothing of Tuigi, at the next table. He stretches his mouth open like the curtain at the movies, enjoys himself. He points at Rebecca on the stage: "That bitch is somethin' else," he says to me.

This Rebecca is attempting a psychedelic dance, her half-naked body, vigorous, smooth, is divided into sections. Below her waist whirls an old-fashioned pocket watch. Her hands row an imaginary boat (they move from front to back, pushing her forward). Her phono-mime of the sexual act seduces everyone's eye, dampens groins, raises hands in applause.

"That bitch is really hot," says Enrique. "She oughta listen to me, pull outa this country before she rots."

I indicate agreement, I feel removed. I establish the coordinates of her type; she'd be a hit in Paris, London, or New York. I expound: I don't recommend South America, limited market, tough competition, lots of cheap ass, a surplus of Cubans after Castro, a common typology—idiocies I don't agree with even as I say them: "By all means," I add, "she should go to Europe."

"Pigalle, Moulin Rouge, Montmartre, too much, a Panamanian in Paris, it's the fuckin' end," says Enrique, revealing the screen, opening the curtains of his mouth.

The applause, hands against hands (Rebecca's act is beyond stagecraft), agitates the mini-world created by sighs and hanging jaws when the dancer begins her exit through a door at the side of the stage.

Enrique takes advantage of the lull filled with the MC's voice to tell me about Ana. He says she is sick. He went to visit her (as always, he is emphatic), and he did not see any sign of sickness to explain her absence. That interest in Ana's health (not at all sudden) surprises me.

All at once, without going any further in his report, Enrique appears frozen, superimposed, incrusted, between Ana and what I desire. He has the look of a winner; he has class. I understand his extroverted, cyclothymic stature; the kind of man who can extract precious metals from the living rock. His expression, and what it communicates, is exaggerated. His aim is to be the sun in whose orbits whirl all the changes that have ever been and will ever be. Now I imagine him stuffed into a bikini, replacing Tuigi, behind the placard on stage inventing a way to let himself be seen, in front of the microphone, taking Ana's place.

My thesis is confirmed little by little. It's hard to believe. In Ana's world, Enrique is a presence. Being certain about that confuses and elates me. Now I can establish my strategy, my defenses, my attacks. It's not the same as moving ahead blindly, willy-nilly. Enrique brings with him a value that is unknown to me, and for some reason this suggests Ana; they are congruent. I am an impostor, a parvenu with nowhere to go, a novice posing as a priest without a parish. "Enrique takes care of her," says Nicho. He tries to block my assault; his tone betrays the fidelity of a dog.

Enrique can't keep still. He drums on the table with his fingers, he taps his feet. A girl from Ecuador with the face of a Peruvian Indian tries out a Mexican *corrido* with a typically Panamanian accent, and Enrique's authentic howls, sobs, cries, captivate the audience. (I look at the Ecuadorianperuvianmexicanpanamanian, my hair standing on end, hating her.) He's off like a comet, kisses a nameless chorus girl on the cheek, greets other courtesans at other tables and with other men, as if they were his guests, in an ostentatious demonstration of the exemplary, single-minded pimp.

"Did you put Ana down on your list?" asks Nicho, taking advantage of Enrique's lingering hyperactivity with Tuigi, Rebecca, Big Butt, Shake It, and the rest, caught in the night with their recalcitrant, drunken clients.

"I have no list," I reply. I am annoyed by his fawning tone, his feline, unyielding attitude. "Maybe one day. I don't think she can satisfy me."

"You don't think what?"

"Just what I said."

"You like the bitch, dontcha?"

"So so."

"I don't get it."

"It's simple. It can't be done just any old way. Not without some agreement, some kind of foundation."

Nicho squints down at me, depraved. He weighs the meaning of what I've said.

"Choosy?"

"Maybe."

Rosa comes to the table with a drink for Nicho; she stole it from the bureaucrats' bottle. She tries to listen. She strings words together, joins them, puts in her two cents intuitively with feigned indifference. She affirms pure innocence between Ana and Enrique.

"They're just friends," she says.

She fills in the picture: an only child, spoiled, misunderstood, wild, a romantic kidder, irresponsible, a drinker, a nice guy, and, for these reasons, Ana doesn't take him

121

seriously. Rosa's confidential tone troubles me, betrays me, undermines my defenses, the I-don't-give-a-damn attitude I want to show, hooray for life and another round of drinks, in that ring where there's no referee and my poker hand is lousy. Basically, Rosa sympathizes with me, thinks she is doing me a stupendous favor.

III

I'm tempted to not go on with the game; my moves are limited. I'm not accepted despite the weeks I've spent on this. I feel like a pawn in a chess game, doomed to lose his head for the sake of a king and the freewheeling strides of a queen (Queen Ana with tights, microphones, chips) over rooks, bishops and knights. In vain I try to make a date outside that universe, so much her own, a rubber ball in her hands, sugar and honey drowning in oceans of Johnnie Walker and footlights. She can understand my perplexity. How useless it is to invent horizons and dovecots, to cut hearts pierced by arrows into the bark of trees, draw fish on the sand, throw a stone at the pelicans, walk barefoot together over twilit lichens, climb to the top of the orange trees to contemplate the empty nests, the wrecked time of melancholy. She rejects that stupid world. She is concrete, practical. She stays away from that childish territory because she fears blindness, the abyss hidden in all simplicity. "You are a mole," I told her, and she looked at me scornfully, cruelly disdainful, as only a natural prostitute can be. Still, she doesn't end it. Contemptuously she comes over to me, drinks the liquor I pay for, leaves the keys to her house on the table so that I won't leave, forces my surrender.

She isn't here today either. She hasn't come after seven days of discouraging and joyful absence. A traffic light in my head warns caution, calm down, stop. Her not being here allows a certain rejoicing, allows me to mount an offensive in the underground war, take over a plaza, tie up loose ends, look into things. I sit down at the table in the back, almost at the same instant Nicho and Rosa (I imagine a celestial mechanism, chalky or muddy, governing the movements of those human dragonflies) come over. They continue talking, drunken, loud—something or other about the rent for the apartment, how little mutual independence they have, the landlord's demands, the need to cut a number from the show because Tuigi is vomiting in the bathroom, one of them has to pay the electric bill, in brief, about which of them should shut up. I watch them. Rosa finally gets up (I imagine an excuse) and sits at a table with two customers.

"To hell with her," says Nicho. "Too much pig and no lard."

"She tries," I say, pointing at Rosa, flirtatious, smiling, at the other table.

A night looms like all the rest, monotonous (fish in the tank, tiger in the zoo, bird in the wicker cage), far from any immensity of sea, jungle or air, next to this novice pimp, sheep in wolf's clothing. Nothing to do or even to hope for, I take my pleasure in the apish, phosphorescent, hallucinatory figures painted, like murals, by anonymous artists on the walls of the *boîte*. Then I ask about Ana.

Nicho—apprentice pimp, whoremaster, mechanic, drunk—plants his elbows on the table, lifts his hands to his eyes as if he were looking for a tiny, microscopic speck, a spring that won't tighten, a gear without teeth. He moves his head from side to side in planetary motion, leans forward, blinks like the windshield wipers of a car.

"Is it true that you haven't . . . ?" he asks, making a sexual gesture with his hands.

"No," I answer. I reveal a little more of my failure at seduction. It doesn't matter. I watch myself playing the worst part in that play, not a parasite, not an imbecile, not a wisecracking john, but the worst part.

"You're fucked, Julio," he says. "El Quique (he was referring to Enrique) took off with Ana over the weekend, you know. If he likes her, she'll stay, official, salary and everything. If you still want to—" he repeated the gesture with his hands "—you'll have to come up with the bread, pay through the nose. You were suckered, brother."

He says all this slowly, emphatically, chewing on each word as if along with the duty to inform there was also pleasure, orgasm, the fullness of life, relief from black nausea in the neck of a bottle.

Tonight the show goes on earlier than usual. The waiter replaces the bowl of cracked ice, the glasses are filled again, emptied and filled, emptied and filled, and the girls, at a signal from the stage manager, leave the tables (not without first asking the customers to wait for them), go into the dressing room, and in a matter of minutes strip off their outer garments and in orderly fashion begin to file onto the stage.

Translated by Edith Grossman

A March Guayacan

Bertalicia Peralta

The night was steamy, and the air that passed through the openings in the wall came in hot, hot like the blood of the townspeople. Dorinda wasn't asleep. She was thinking, wasn't dreaming. Sometimes she dreamed. Dreamed about the beautiful and sweet things she never had. She wasn't dreaming now. Nor sleeping. Just thinking. And the thoughts turned tumbleweeding in her mind, parched her mind; then suddenly they made the black almond eyes shine. She moved on the cot. It was a light movement. Even so, the man at her side seemed to feel it because he curled up tighter and tried to snuggle up. Dorinda cringed away. She felt an awesome loathing for that tough, sweaty body that for so many years had stayed on top of hers, against hers, squeezing the breasts, thighs, panting over her belly, ripping her sex, opening her always, opening her, trying to destroy her, she thought. She moved to the other end of the cot.

"Let's go dance," he had said one day some time before. She just looked at him. What did he want? "Let's go," he insisted.

She didn't go. Who would take care of the three little angels she had in the house? There were more than a few stories in the town about irresponsible mothers who had gone dancing, abandoned their children, left them alone, and then something terrible happened to them. Some were hurt. One had a house burn down with the little ones locked up inside for safety's sake; some brute knocked up a child only five or six. No. She didn't go. She had to take care of the children.

But other dances came along, other get-togethers. He was always after her. She felt a distrust in the very beginning which became a sort of habit. She got used to his being around, even though there were many things she didn't like about him. His habit of fighting with her kids, who were not his. His resentment when he saw them, when he spoke to them. And then his guile and cunning attitude to pretend when he could see she had noticed he was coming up with the same old story. It was like playing the fox and the hen. She felt he wanted her for himself, and so he would deceive her, showing her that he liked the kids. But she knew he didn't.

And the booze. When he was sober he worked hard. He took the lumps. He even had his good-natured moments of tenderness—languid eyes that preceded getting into her on some wooded hill, the pleasures under a cloudless sky, the tussles and horseplay quite a distance from the house. He liked it this way. Until he maneuvered his way into her house, and they lived together and were very happy. No. Dorinda laughed under her breath. "And they lived happily ever after" was the ending to stories they always read in school, many years ago when she was a child and her grandmother sent her to school up to the second grade. Happy, yes, let's not deny it, sometimes, a little. When he got paid, when they went to some dance, and when he embraced her gently before he drank himself under the table. But it lasted too briefly. As he drank, he'd go out of his head, squashed her between his arms, only to keep from falling, the good-for-nothing. And he was jealous of all the other men. At some arbitrary moment she'd have to go home alone and wait for him to arrive, a brute, to drop on her without feeling, going soft, falling asleep because he was so drunk. He didn't stir until the day was in full swing with the sun on high.

Dorinda got up and left the house. It was cooler outside. March made a hot terrain, a hot breeze, hot blood. She looked for a little water in a jar. It was cool in terra cotta. The worst was when he made up the thing about children. Now he wanted children—*his* children because the others were not. And she knew he hated them. Above all the little girl. And she was not about to have more children. She had found out all the details at the clinic. The doctor had counseled her, and now she knew what she had to do. But though she tried hard not to, she became pregnant again. She didn't tell him anything, but he could tell. Her belly started to stretch, the breasts to fill, the eyes to sink deeper. He knew. And he told the whole world. Then he went on a week-long binge.

"So we are going to have more children in the family, Dorinda?" asked her neighbors.

"Don't believe him, they are just stories," she had said.

"Hmm, and what about that swelling in the belly? About three months along, No?"

She answered, "No, I say. I won't have any more."

Dorinda breathed in the night's cool breeze. The sky was dark, not a single star. A splendid darkness covered the entire land as she gathered her hair into a topknot.

"Why did you spread the news?" she asked the man. "I won't have any more children. I'm going to abort." She said this haltingly, pensively. The other three were outside the house. He was stretched out in the hammock, smoking. She ground corn, slowly, rhythmically, her belly rubbing against the rim of the basin. Her arms lifted and fell with strength, with certainty.

"Are you crazy?" And without giving her a chance to suspect it, he leaped up looming over her, grabbed her by the shoulders, whirled her around, and with his eyes ablaze, looking at her like a beast, he said: "Are you crazy? If you go through with it, I'll kill you. I'll kill you," and off he went.

He got soused that night, once again. And he touted on and on. For the first time Dorinda felt afraid. He would do it. He was a brute, and he would go through with it. He was a brute, and he couldn't see that there wasn't enough of anything around the house. That she worked all day and practically all night. It didn't matter to him. "Anyway, they're not my kids," he'd always say. And the kids grew, and they'd have to go to school. All of it. It wasn't true that they were going to be ignoramuses like he and she. She started to think. She calculated day and night. She began to take stock of the advantages she had with him. She had none. To the contrary. She had aged ten years in the two gone by since the first night he'd moved into her house.

Dorinda set out slowly by herself, headed for the creek in the gorge drying up in the summer heat. She did everything as she'd been told. The creek took away the blood flowing from her sex while she strained squatting.

Then she lay on the grass to regain her strength. Impetuous tears spilled uncontrollably, blurred her sight, burned her eyes as if salt had been thrown into them. She screamed. She felt such a deep sadness—something between grief and shame—so intensely hers, a sadness that had always been there, so much so she had never noticed it. She cried until she felt free. She got up and took her time getting back to the house.

The man was sleeping. She had set it up this way. Not even a fire would rouse him. The kids weren't there. They'd been sent to her sister's "so they could get to know their cousins better," as if this were a necessity of some kind. Dorinda approached the cot. The man was sweating. She recalled the times he had sweated over her, trying to get at her very guts. She wouldn't be missed at all. She had never been needed, truly, within his reality. She knew him well. He was a tough character. If he said he'd kill her, he would do it. But she wasn't going to let him. No. Not anymore. Now at this point, Dorinda would no longer permit some things in life. Not a soul knew any of this. She approached the man. She poked him. She tugged at him. She pushed him. He felt lifeless. But she knew he was alive. He was just out cold.

Calmly she went into the kitchen. She picked up a knife and gripped it firmly by the handle. She thrust it into the heart of the man more than once. The blood ran in torrents, first streaming, then more slowly until it stopped. A lot of blood. It smelled. She made sure he was dead. She thrust the knife three more times into the body.

The night was still hot and dark. Then she closed the windows and turned on a lamp very low. She tried to move the corpse, but she realized that it was too heavy for her alone. She relaxed and began to carve up the body. First the head, then the arms, the legs. Piece by piece. When she had all of it in small pieces, she stuffed them into a hemp sack and tied it up with bejuco reed. She dragged it outside the house. She went after the horse and strapped on the cinch. Mounting the horse, she pulled the hemp sack to the pasture over the hill.

When she got there her face was cool. Her deep-set eyes had their usual mysterious brilliance. She dug out a hole as deep as she could. Her body was used to the hard work of the countryside, and it obeyed her cerebral impulses. She put the hemp sack into the ground and threw dirt on it. She planted a *guayacán* and went back to the house. She spent the rest of the night cleaning up every spot of blood very carefully. She was bothered by the odor that seemed to permeate the dirt floor, the walls and cot.

Morning came clear and radiant. Dorinda was up early and went to the creek in the gorge to wash her sheets. She met other women there.

"Dorinda, what about the little baby?" one of them asked.

"Didn't I tell you that was pure gossip," she answered. "There's not a man who's going to make me pregnant."

"And Jacinto?" they asked, only to go on talking about something while beating the clothes against the rocks.

"He left at daybreak," said Dorinda. "He told me he was going to see if he could find work in the Canal Zone. If he doesn't find anything, he'll hop a ship as a seaman. Perhaps, he'll never come back."

Since it was March and Dorinda hoped the *guayacán* would grow tall and full of flowers, every day she went with her children to water the small tree.

Translated by Zoë Anglesey

Microbus to
San Salvador

Manlio Argueta

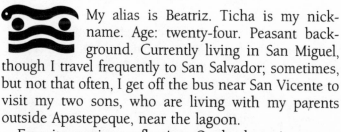 My alias is Beatriz. Ticha is my nickname. Age: twenty-four. Peasant background. Currently living in San Miguel, though I travel frequently to San Salvador; sometimes, but not that often, I get off the bus near San Vicente to visit my two sons, who are living with my parents outside Apastepeque, near the lagoon.

Favorite pastime: reflection. Or daydreaming, some people call it.

Element of nature which is special to me: *metate*. It's a precious stone, made from the lava of volcanoes; my parents, grandparents, and great-grandparents all made a living from it. They made grinding stones. For grinding corn. We peasants grind corn using the strength of our arms. On a *metate* base shaped like a small washtub, using a pestle, also made of *metate*, we mash corn that has been cooked in water and ashes. The ashes help to soften it. After a few pounds of the pestle, which is also called the handstone, the corn becomes a spongy white dough, which has a pleasant feel and a very agreeable taste. That's what we peasants live on. We form the dough into a tortilla by kneading it with our fingers and palms, then we put it over the fire on a *comal*, or clay griddle. The tortilla is our bread. It is life.

No peasant home is without a grindstone. I used to help my parents make grindstones. That's why *metate* is my favorite stone. The flower I prefer is mignonette.

I wonder where we would be without corn. Nowhere. We eat tortillas with salt our whole life. We *campesinos*, peasants. I grew up on them. We live and love on them. Sometimes there are beans. We also eat leaves, a lot of leaves; flowers of all kinds; the top shoot of certain plants, especially pines; and herbs, quite a few herbs. Also, we run across small game every now and then: *garrobo* lizards, iguanas, rabbits, coati, *pacas*; or *tacuacines*, which are large rodents that are very good to eat, seeing as nobody eats their chickens anymore.

But we like tortillas with salt best of all. There wouldn't be a meal without them. Anyway, that's all we need to fill us up. Because, of course, that's all there is.

To us, life is a miracle of God.

Living is something else: keeping your body free of disease, not dying from rickets or diarrhea; or starvation. Over half the small children in a given family die from these causes.

Maybe that's why we always want big families. It's a kind of defense to keep the race alive. Besides, the more hands a family has, the better its chances to earn its daily bread.

We must also survive. That's something else again.

They're after us. The authorities haven't been able to even look at a peasant since 1932 without being filled with rage. Now, half a century later, things have gotten out of control. There are no jails. If you fall into the hands of the law, you're dead. They say our country is too small for the amount of people who live here. People who say that have studied abroad, or they're foreigners who support the authorities. The government says it too. They claim there are too many of us, that's what the problem is. They teach that in the military academy. The advisers teach it. I don't know how they rationalize it, but from time to time they shout: You're a plague, you poor people are a curse from God. People were happy before Cuzcatlán got populated. You've been multiplying, like the fish and loaves. It's time to wipe out poverty. They say it in a way that makes it sound pretty.

However, we live by the strength of our hands and produce the wealth that those who are well-off possess. The rich used to be happy. Not anymore. It's our fault. That's how a lot of professional soldiers—those who have studied in military schools both here and abroad—put it. Because the advisers are the same way.

The advisers don't know anything about us. That's the problem. They come to our country in big airplanes. They tour the countryside in their helicopters. They wear dark glasses so they can't see our light. They drive bulletproof Cherokees. They don't speak Spanish. How are they going to understand us like that?

They are happy. We survive.

They're after us. They murder us. The most common cause of death for someone like me is decapitation. Dismemberment. Just as the conquistadors did five hundred years ago. They used to threaten you with jail. Every estate, every hacienda, had its own jail. Whenever a person didn't want to work for the *patrón*, the owner of the estate, he was jailed as a vagrant and a troublemaker. There's still a law against vagrants and troublemakers, but it no longer applies. Now they apply a swift death instead. If the advisers knew our history, would they still treat us the same? I don't know. Besides, our history is sad and boring. Maybe they're not interested in hearing about it. We're interested, though, because it gives us strength. It teaches us to survive.

We've learned how to survive. That's why I use an alias.

I have two sons. I will never have a big family. I don't live with them right now. They live with my parents in a hamlet near Apastepeque. And my grandmother lived just a few miles from there, north of the lagoon. For a long time, before I was born, my grandparents lived on the south shore, but it was flooded and they were forced to move. They planted annatto trees and beans on a little parcel there, together with their children and Grandma's father, Emiliano. For a while they made a living making grindstones and selling things like cottage cheese and *conserva de leche*, or milk pudding. Recently, they decided to abandon the grindstone trade. People weren't buying them anymore. Since the stones lasted for many, many years, longer than a lifetime, people stopped buying them. Everybody already had one. My family sold them. They've had them in their huts since my great-great-grandfather's time, and they treat them like jewels. That was a problem, so we had to give up the trade: the stones lasted forever.

I always got along well with my grandmother. She died a few months ago. She was sixty. It's her name I use as my alias. She's a symbol for me. You wouldn't think that with the age difference and the distance between us I would take her name. But it's symbolic. Her name was Beatriz.

Besides our ages, there were other differences between us. She never left her hamlet, never cared for cities. I did, because one day I decided to leave the zone of Apastepeque; in essence, I was following in the footsteps of my older sister Antonia. It was actually my father's aunt who got us to leave home; she took us to work with her in a cooperative in Chalate. This aunt was my godmother. "You must come with me," she said, "so you can have a better life." And so you can survive.

I was forced to take the children to live with my parents when my *compañero*, their father, died. I realized it would be impossible to take care of them. They went back to the place of my birth. I don't know what will become of them.

When my *compa* was alive, we took turns looking after the kids. I worked in the Social Improvement Textile Factory, which was run by the government in San Miguel before they turned it into a garrison. Now you can't even use that street to get to the train station if you want to go to Colonia Belén. At night I had plenty of time to study the principles of nursing—we called it first aid—which was a course given by the trade union. And my *compa* was involved in his own affairs, though I was never quite sure what they were. I did know that he hadn't worked in the factory for over two years because they fired him for being a union member. We got along all right, living and surviving. He went under an assumed name like me.

When the factory became a garrison, we were all laid off. No severance pay, nothing. The union helped out a lot, though, because we decided to keep it going even though the factory no longer existed, so we went to San Salvador to the Ministry of Labor to see if they wouldn't give us at least enough to live on for a month.

That was our excuse to stay organized. Because once they fire you, forget it. You could drop dead asking for handouts. So we didn't press too hard, but we did have an excuse to get together and go to San Salvador to meet with other trade unions. And that's how I got so deeply involved in the struggle. I had some previous experience from the cooperatives in Chalate, which was good because it helped me learn what it means to defend your rights.

Once they killed my *compañero*, things changed. I couldn't keep on living in San Miguel with my children. My reputation as a union member and the wife of a slain worker was a direct threat. I explained the situation to my parents and they understood. So did my grandmother. The little ones could live in both places. It was barely an hour's walk between them.

Together we'll fight the war.

If I hadn't been organized, I would have wound up dead like thousands of other people. The vast majority of the forty thousand people killed in the last three years are innocent. It's part of the extermination plan.

I don't include myself among the innocent. I try and fight back, so that's why I use an assumed name and do other things. We're at war. If I hadn't left the hamlet, I wouldn't really have known what was going on. I would have been a victim. Thanks to my father's aunt, we're advancing and seeing life in a different way. Both my sister Antonia and I. We both went to Chalate. We worked in a cooperative there; but to get organized we went to San Miguel. Fleeing practically.

That woman was very advanced. I never would have guessed. My father's aunt.

You never know when you'll get caught by the authorities. They're strong. Maybe stronger than we are because they don't have to hide or use assumed names. We have to, in order to survive.

We do have one big advantage: we've organized ourselves. That's where we excel. And in conscience, too.

Sometimes I think this whole life is a dream.

After being away for a few years, I have to go back to Chalate for a couple of days; they have asked me to identify someone whose name doesn't even deserve to be mentioned. We'd like to be forgiving. We're an emotional people, maybe because of the life we lead. They show us only their cruel side to arouse our feelings. They think if they take their rage out on us, our contempt will turn to hate, and then they'll have an excuse to exterminate us. That's been the authorities' policy for the last three years. If we speak out, they kill us. If we're suspected of speaking out, they disappear us. And if we keep our mouths shut, they think we're hiding something. So they kill us for that, too. We used to have a right to remain silent, at least. Now they make us talk so we don't keep our hatred to ourselves. Then they have another excuse to kill us. "Everything that moves in the zone is suspicious," the military chief has told the pilots who drop bombs from their airplanes. We even have to be careful about the way we look at people. We have to choke back the tears for our dead. If we mourn them, that makes us their accomplices. So we get killed. The key is to learn how to hide your emotions. That's very characteristic of this war. We're not even allowed to cry.

So I don't know what will happen when I meet Corporal Martínez, prisoner of the guerrillas in Chalate. I have to give testimony on him. That's where I'm going, to Chalate. It's a difficult situation. Though they say people are at their best when things get tough.

I've always enjoyed reflection. I think of it as a way to live two lives. Especially now that the authorities show no mercy and use us as targets for their new weapons, which we've never seen before.

I'd rather forget Corporal Martínez. And think about my *compañero* instead, about the last time we traveled together on this same microbus. He really gives me strength and confidence. He was like a brother. I liked it that way. We lived through a lot of hard times and a lot of separations. One time he was gone for six months. Without a word. But I knew nothing would happen to him. Because he was working for our survival.

The last time I saw him we were together on the bus.

To tell the truth, it's very sad being alone with nothing but a shadow or the thought of him suddenly appearing with the same old smile and greeting, carrying a couple of oranges in a plastic bag.

I was just thinking—not about the last time I saw him but about the time he disappeared for six months. We didn't have any children yet. It's harder to be alone when you don't have children.

Always waiting for him to appear. I got far in my first-aid studies. Without a husband or kids around I had time to spare. Each night when I came back to our room at the hostel, I hoped he would be there to surprise me—sitting quietly on one of our two stools, like all the times before, waiting to pick me up and hug me, and then we'd squeeze each other tight, never wanting to let go, and we'd walk together still clinging to one another. Then I'd stand on his feet and he'd spin me around the room. Both of us laughing wildly. We could stay that way for a long time.

But he wouldn't be there. And I'd be filled with sadness. Those were six desperate months. Now, to think we'll never be together again. Not me or his two children. Separated for the rest of our lives.

It took a lot out of me to give my kids to my parents; but they understood. My *compañero* was dead, and there was no way I could keep them in my room and take care of them—I was working both at the factory and for the union.

The day he was killed, we were traveling on the bus together. He was only going as far as San Vicente, and I was going all the way to San Salvador, because we were on two separate assignments.

It was just a mile or two to the San Vicente stop, where he would get off and continue on foot into the city—there was a mile and a half to go on the highway when the microbus was pulled over by a patrol. There were over a hundred *guardias* hidden on a side road with "Mazinger" trucks.

It's an awful experience running into them. You never know what they'll do next. They told the driver to pull over. We thought they would search us. I made a mental note of the contents of my purse: I had my identification card, a picture I took in Barrios Park, San Miguel, with my two kids, a couple of centavos, and all the other odds and ends you carry around for goodness knows what reason. I felt better.

My *compa* and I were sitting together without saying a word. Like total strangers. When the patrol surprised us like that, coming around the bend, we thought they'd open fire and people got nervous. My *compa* took my hand and surreptitiously slipped it around his waist. This surprised me. But then I realized what he was doing, because I felt a metallic object beneath his shirt. I squeezed his hand for several seconds to let

139

him know I didn't want him to shoot it and get killed. What could he do, anyway? He let go of my hand when he knew I'd found the weapon. Clutching his hand for those few seconds made me feel like they would never end. Life walks right up and slaps you, just like that. Standing on his feet, whirling around the room, holding on to each other. For dear life, so nothing would break us apart.

We have a humble home. A single room with a hallway leading out to a patio surrounded by other run-down rooms—communal toilets right there in the middle of the patio, which is how you can tell it's a *mesón*, a hostel. Our room is big enough to fit a bed, a pinewood table, and two stools. On the table there's an instant-coffee container filled with some crepe paper flowers: a vase. There's also a closet which we bought with our savings after our first year in San Miguel. The closet is divided in half. On one side there are a few shelves, and on the other there's a pole for hanging dresses and shirts; below, there are two drawers to which my *compañero* added false bottoms for storing sensitive documents. Hanging from a nail on the wall is a print of a little boy with curly hair holding a globe in his left hand; his right is near his heart giving the sign of benediction; there's a halo over his head and a slight smile on his face; a white tunic hangs from one of his shoulders; the other is bare. He is *El Salvador del Mundo*, the Savior of the World. Between the curly haired boy and the cardboard backing that holds him in the wooden frame there is another, hidden print of Monsignor Romero.

We keep it hidden in order not to cause problems with the authorities; it could cost us a disappearance into one of their subterranean jails.

The hallway leading to the patio is divided by a newspaper-covered partition, and that's where we keep a kerosene stove.

We lived in that room for almost six years. Both our kids were born there. Mesón Las Flores, San Miguel.

We were happy at the *mesón*. Despite the fact my *compañero* occasionally had to leave for long periods of time on union business. But I knew he'd come back sooner or later, even if he'd been gone for months. He'd always come back at night, knocking three times with a long pause between each knock. I opened the door and he stood there, not coming in; he just looked at me, hunting me down with his eyes and his smile. I, the nervous doe. Whenever we got together again, we played this happy game for the first few seconds. Then he came in, took my head in one hand, and closed the door with the other. We never took our eyes off one another. We never stopped smiling. And the minute the door was shut, we'd leap into each other's arms.

We were lucky to have a room on the street. It was better for catching the breezes that blew through the open door. It's hot in San Miguel. So nobody closes doors facing the street. That way everybody knows everybody else, because no one can hide behind four walls.

We were happy there. And scared sometimes, because we weren't natives and it took a while to adjust to the way people did things: you had to let your neighbors know everything you were doing that day—where are you going, where have you been, what did you do there, can I help you, let me come along, I'll join you, what's your name, would you like a piece of sweetbread, may I borrow a pinch of salt. In other words, all the things that make you feel a part of the community—making contact, talking in doorways, on the street, at the corner. People think you're strange if you keep to yourself. People like us who were involved in union activities after work had to tell our neighbors at the *mesón* that we'd be late, but we'd be back by such and such a time. And then I had to explain my *compañero*'s long absences. Naturally we were always making things up.

But from another point of view, it's an advantage, it's not so hard to be alone. In fact, you're never alone. You just have to get used to it. You get to know people and you realize they don't mean to pry, they just want to help. In spite of the difficulties, we liked San Miguel. We were happy as long as we could be together. The long separations didn't matter. They made us feel that much closer. It was a terrible blow. If it wasn't for our two sons, I would never have gotten over his death. And that wouldn't have been good, because it would have affected my work and my prospects.

Translated by Clark Hansen

Sodom

Samuel Rovinski

 In the next room, the lamentations were so heart-rending they made the walls weep a heavy dampness.

Motl raised his eyes from his plate and stared at his mother's hands as they steadily peeled an onion. He wanted to make a comment, but decided to say nothing and finish the rest of the omelette. Besides, his coffee was getting cold.

Now they were moans.

His father, rocking in a worn wicker chair, made an authoritative gesture followed by a furious look.

Motl stood up, his wide hips dragging the chair after him for a moment. He was sweating on this May morning, and his soul hardened when he thought of her.

He went into the next room, shouted something incomprehensible, returned to the kitchen, and fell heavily into the chair. The sobbing subsided as Motl sipped his coffee. Now he was satisfied, and his father buried himself in his reading of the Yiddish newspaper.

The thin wooden walls filled with a heavy silence, hardly broken by the knife as it cut the onion against the ochre of the kitchen sink. But the silence was no longer silence in Motl's head. He saw the woman sprawled in bed like a whining animal, and the accusing glance that followed him down the stairs, along the street, and into the leather shop.

He looked at his mother with great tenderness; he compared her to the other one, and once again he repented of his marriage.

"Mama," he said, as he carried his cup and plate to the sink, "don't go to the market. Let that bitch go when she gets up!"

His mother agreed with a vague gesture and began to cut another onion into thin slices.

He approached the old man warily. "Tata, have you finished?"

The old man pointed to the lower part of his trousers. Motl detached the little bottle, with its straw-colored liquid, and went to empty it in the toilet. He came back, lumbering like a whale calf, reattached the bottle to his father's belly, said good-bye to both of them, and left for the leather shop.

In the street he was approached, as always, by the prostitutes from the cheap hotel next door, more for the sake of mocking his slow timidity and his fat flabby body than to lure him into one of the sordid rooms in the labyrinth of infamy that Motl imagined.

As he opened the padlock and raised the rusted metal that barred the door of the leather shop, his hairy skin sweated with dread at the thought of the tales of lust and crime that Juancito, the clerk, would bring him today, as he did every day.

"The world is corrupt," he said to himself bitterly, "and there is no salvation."

He made his daily inventory of the skins and felt relief at finding everything in order. Gently, he breathed in the faint odor of animality and tannin on the skins that were stacked on the shelves of the shop. This shop had made his father rich and would belong to him someday when the cancer finally killed off his tyrannical authority.

At noon his mother came in, wrapped in the submissive silence of an act she had been repeating since the days of the dim past. Without saying a word, looking at Motl out of the corner of her eye, she left the lunch pail on the counter and waited a few moments, barely long enough for her son to give her the money for marketing and a kiss on her cheek.

Motl ate facing the calendar with the photograph of the naked woman, sweating in the intense midday heat, goaded by a strange uneasiness that clouded his thoughts. He daydreamed about the city of sin until his father came in.

It rained heavily that afternoon.

Father and son hardly spoke. Juancito waited on the shoemakers who came in for skins, tacks, nails, and glue, with his habitual lightheartedness and the shameless language of the place, which was absolutely indecipherable to the old man's understanding and Motl's indifference.

The weather cleared, and the city was enveloped in the golden tints of dusk. It was time to close the leather shop.

When the first star appeared, father and son went to say the evening prayers at the improvised synagogue in the store across the street, where they could barely manage to bring together the ten men required by Jewish law.

Between the prayer that ends the day and the one that begins the night, Motl prayed to God to cleanse the world of the sins of the flesh. And he returned home with the hope that he would not find her there anymore, that the wind would have blown her away.

Again he walked past the scandalous women from the cheap hotel, and he swelled with faith in divine wrath, savoring with anticipation the spectacle of death and destruction in the corrupt city, ready to settle accounts with her too, the bitch.

Thinking about the miracle, he opened the street door to walk into the living room, which he expected to find empty of her presence. But the woman was there, sitting on the old leather chair, draped in lust and smiling the enigmatic smile that Motl loathed so deeply.

It was his entrance into hell. He felt suffocated in the air heavy with the strong animal odor radiating from the woman, clouding the good smell of the leather.

He filled with rage when he saw her eating chocolates with a defiant look. At that moment he could have killed her, but his father came in after him without taking off his hat or saying a word to the woman, as if she did not exist, and pulled him by the arm toward the dining room where his mother and the account books were waiting for them.

Motl smelled infidelity in the woman's cheap perfume and seductive dress. She was plump and indolent. And indolence is the root of all vice, as everyone knows, just as the act of devouring chocolates from morning to night shows a will to depravity.

He hated her for that and for many other things that he could not explain. In his heart of hearts he reproached his parents for having chosen her to be his wife and thus disturbing the sweet harmony that had always reigned in the house. That woman was the vehicle for all the lasciviousness in the world, the Trojan horse that had shattered the security of his home.

146

They sat down to eat. His father blessed the table, and they ate copiously until they were satisfied. All except the woman, who looked at them mockingly, licking her fingers that were soaked with the cherry liquor that oozed out of the chocolates.

Motl stood up heavily and went to the bathroom to hide from the indecent image that filled him with nausea. Then he felt overwhelmed by lethargy, and he decided to go to his room.

He undressed quickly, with the light off so that he would not see himself, even by chance, and he collapsed into bed, squeezing his eyes shut.

Then she came in, along with the obscene noises that poured in from the other side of the wall: the whispers, the laughter, the monstrous panting from the shabby cubicles of the brothel. She, like them, took her clothes off slowly in order to weaken him.

He thought of his parents and God and the Angel who would come to save him, and he closed his eyes so that he would not catch sight of the swelling breasts and curving hips of the woman who came under his blanket, naked like a Lilith rising out of hell.

Motl felt that he had been deceived. All that was left of the chaste and deeply pious woman whom they had brought to his house was this malevolent, voluptuous, lustful sorceress who did not let him breathe in that narrow bed, just as his imaginings of the immoral acts committed in the brothel did not let him breathe.

Lilith had to disappear along with all other lewdness in the city, so that righteous conduct among men and faith in God could be reestablished once more.

Motl felt that a miracle was near. The voice of the Most High was about to shake the foundations of the temple that housed the priestesses of the Evil One.

The two angels had scoured the city and had not found the just man they were searching for, and they deemed it necessary to bury it under a rain of burning oil and pitch so that all traces of hateful sin would be completely eradicated. But the All Powerful ordered a new search, and the angels returned to the city.

Motl did not allow himself to be moved by Lilith's provocative advances. As always, ever since his wedding night, he refused to respond to her. He felt nothing for her but hatred and a desire to beat her. The more she rubbed herself against his back, mouthing filthy words, the greater was his impulse to hurt her.

He felt repugnance for the repetition of an act that by now had become ritual, but he convinced himself that it was necessary so that he could recapture the dream and prepare an auspicious welcome for the coming of the angels.

He stretched out his hand and found the leather strap, and then he turned to her so that he could whip her like a dog.

When the moaning stopped and Motl was calm once more, after a spasm of pleasure, the city lay submerged in a disquieting silence that was like an omen of fearful events to come.

At that moment, as his soul seemed to float in nothingness and time stopped to recapitulate the All, Motl saw them appear in the doorway, bathed in a cold blue light.

They spoke, but the world did not tremble and the city did not sink into Chaos.

Motl knew then that he was not the chosen one and that he was obliged to continue his life. When he opened his eyes to the first light of dawn and the sounds of the sinful city, he saw her, still sleeping, smiling her eternal enigmatic smile.

Translated by Edith Grossman

And We Sold
the Rain

Carmen Naranjo

"This is a royal fuck-up," was all the treasury minister could say a few days ago as he got out of the jeep after seventy kilometers of jouncing over dusty rutted roads and muddy trails. His advisor agreed: there wasn't a cent in the treasury, the line for foreign exchange wound four times around the capital, and the IMF was stubbornly insisting that the country could expect no more loans until the interest had been paid up, public spending curtailed, salaries frozen, domestic production increased, imports reduced, and social programs cut.

The poor were complaining, "We can't even buy beans—they've got us living on radish tops, bananas and garbage; they raise our water bills but don't give us any water even though it rains every day, and on top of that they add on a charge for excess consumption for last year, even though there wasn't any water in the pipes then either."

"Doesn't anyone in this whole goddamned country have an idea that could get us out of this?" asked the president of the republic, who shortly before the elections, surrounded by a toothily smiling, impeccably tailored meritocracy, had boasted that by virtue of his university-trained mind (Ph.D. in developmental economics) he was the best candidate. Someone proposed to him that he pray to La Negrita; he did and nothing happened. Somebody else suggested that he reinstate the Virgin of Ujarrás. But after so many years of neglect, the pretty little virgin had gone deaf and ignored the pleas for help, even though the entire cabinet implored her, at the top of their lungs, to light the way to a better future and a happier tomorrow.

The hunger and poverty could no longer be concealed: the homeless, pockets empty, were squatting in the Parque Central, the Parque Nacional, and the Plaza de la Cultura. They were camping along Central and Second Avenues and in a shantytown springing up on the plains outside the city. Gangs were threatening to invade the national theater, the Banco Central, and all nationalized banking headquarters. The Public Welfare Agency was rationing rice and beans as if they were medicine. In the marketplace, robberies increased to one per second, and homes were burgled at the rate of one per half hour. Business and government were sinking in sleaze; drug lords operated uncontrolled, and gambling was institutionalized in order to launder dollars and attract tourists. Strangely enough, the prices of a few items went down: whiskey, caviar and other such articles of conspicuous consumption.

The sea of poverty that was engulfing cities and villages contrasted with the growing number of Mercedes Benzes, BMWs and a whole alphabet of trade names of gleaming new cars.

The minister announced to the press that the country was on the verge of bankruptcy. The airlines were no longer issuing tickets because so much money was owed them, and travel became impossible; even official junkets were eliminated. There was untold suffering of civil servants suddenly unable to travel even once a month to the great cities of the world! A special budget might be the solution, but tax revenues were nowhere to be found, unless a compliant public were to go along with the president's brilliant idea of levying a tax on air—a minimal tax, to be sure, but, after all, the air was a part of the government's patrimony. Ten *colones* per breath would be a small price to pay.

July arrived, and one afternoon a minister without portfolio and without umbrella, noticing that it had started to rain, stood watching people run for cover. "Yes," he thought, "here it rains like it rains in Comala, like it rains in Macondo. It rains day and night, rain after rain, like a theater with the same movie, sheets of water. Poor people without umbrellas, without a change of clothes, they get drenched, people living in leaky houses, without a change of shoes for when they're shipwrecked. And here, all my poor colleagues with colds, all the poor deputies with laryngitis, the president with that worrisome cough, all this on top of the catastrophe itself. No TV station is broadcasting; all of them are flooded, along with the newspaper plants and the radio stations. A people without news is a lost people, because they don't know that everywhere else, or almost everywhere else, things are even worse. If we could only export the rain," thought the minister.

Meanwhile, the people, depressed by the heavy rains, the dampness, the lack of news, the cold, and their hunger and despair without their sitcoms and soap operas, began to rain inside and to increase the baby population—that is, to try to increase the odds that one of their progeny might survive. A mass of hungry, naked babies began to cry in concert every time it rained.

When one of the radio transmitters was finally repaired, the president was able to broadcast a message: He had inherited a country so deeply in debt that it could no longer obtain credit and could no longer afford to pay either the interest or the amortization on loans. He had to dismiss civil servants, suspend public works, cut off services, close offices, and spread his legs somewhat to transnationals. Now even these lean cows were dying; the fat ones were on the way, encouraged by the International Monetary Fund, the AID and the IDB, not to mention the EEC. The great danger was that the fat cows had to cross over the neighboring country on their way, and it was possible that they would be eaten up—even though they came by air, at nine thousand feet above the ground, in a first class stable in a pressurized, air-conditioned cabin. Those neighbors were simply not to be trusted.

The fact was that the government had faded in the people's memory. By now no one remembered the names of the president or his ministers; people remembered them as "the one with glasses who thinks he's Tarzan's mother," or "the one who looks like the baby hog someone gave me when times were good, maybe a little uglier."

The solution came from the most unexpected source. The country had organized the Third World contest to choose "Miss Underdeveloped," to be elected, naturally, from the multitudes of skinny, dusky, round-shouldered, short-legged, half-bald girls with cavity-pocked smiles, girls suffering from parasites and God knows what else. The prosperous Emirate of the

Emirs sent its designée, who in sheer amazement at how it rained and rained, widened her enormous eyes—fabulous eyes of harem and Koran delights— and was unanimously elected reigning Queen of Underdevelopment. Lacking neither eyeteeth nor molars, she was indeed the fairest of the fair. She returned in a rush to the Emirate of the Emirs, for she had acquired, with unusual speed, a number of fungal colonies that were taking over the territory under her toenails and fingernails, behind her ears, and on her left cheek.

"Oh, Father Sultan, my lord, lord of the moons and of the suns, if your Arabian highness could see how it rains and rains in that country, you would not believe it. It rains day and night. Everything is green, even the people; they are green people, innocent and trusting, who probably have never even thought about selling their most important resource, the rain. The poor fools think about coffee, rice, sugar, vegetables, and lumber, and they hold Ali Baba's treasure in their hands without even knowing it. What we would give to have such abundance!"

Sultan Abun dal Tol let her speak and made her repeat the part about the rain from dawn to dusk, dusk to dawn, for months on end. He wanted to hear over and over about that greenness that was forever turning greener. He loved to think of it raining and raining, of singing in the rain, of showers bringing forth flowers . . .

A long distance phone call was made to the office of the export minister from the Emirate of the Emirs, but the minister wasn't in. The trade minister grew radiant when Sultan Abun dal Tol, warming to his subject, instructed him to buy up rain and construct an aqueduct between their countries to fertilize the desert. Another call. Hello, am I speaking with the country of rain, not the rain of marijuana or cocaine, not that of laundered dollars, but the rain that falls naturally from the sky and makes the sandy desert green? Yes, yes, you are speaking with the export minister, and we are willing to sell you our rain. Of course, its production costs us nothing; it is a resource as natural to us as your petroleum. We will make you a fair and just agreement.

The news filled five columns during the dry season, when obstacles like floods and dampness could be overcome. The president himself made the announcement: We will sell rain at ten dollars per cc. The price will be reviewed every ten years. Sales will be unlimited. With the earnings we will regain our independence and our self-respect.

The people smiled. A little less rain would be agreeable to everyone, and the best part was not having to deal with the six fat cows, who were more than a little oppressive. The IMF, the World Bank, the AID, the Embassy, the International Development Bank and perhaps the EEC would stop pushing the cows on them, given the danger that they might be stolen in the neighboring country, air-conditioned cabin, first class stable and all. Moreover, one couldn't count on those cows really being fat, since accepting them meant increasing all kinds of taxes, especially those on consumer goods, lifting import restrictions, spreading one's legs completely open to the transnationals, paying the interest, which was now a little higher, and amortizing the debt that was increasing at a rate only comparable to the spread of an epidemic. And as if this were not enough, it would be necessary to structure the cabinet a certain way, as some ministers were viewed by some legislators as potentially dangerous, as extremists.

The president added with demented glee, his face garlanded in sappy smiles, that French technicians, those guardians of European meritocracy, would build the rain funnels and the aqueduct, a guarantee of honesty, efficiency and effective transfer of technology.

By then we had already sold, to our great disadvantage, the tuna, the dolphins, and the thermal dome, along with the forests and all Indian artifacts. Also our talent, dignity, sovereignty, and the right to traffic in anything and everything illicit.

The first funnel was located on the Atlantic coast, which in a few months looked worse than the dry Pacific. The first payment from the emir arrived—in dollars!—and the country celebrated with a week's vacation. A little more effort was needed. Another funnel was added in the north and one more in the south. Both zones immediately dried up like raisins. The checks did not arrive. What happened? The IMF garnisheed them for interest payments. Another effort: a funnel was installed in the center of the country, where formerly it had rained and rained. It now stopped raining forever, which paralyzed brains, altered behavior, changed the climate, defoliated the corn, destroyed the coffee, poisoned aromas, devastated canefields, dessicated palm trees, ruined orchards, razed truck gardens, and narrowed faces, making people look and act like rats, ants, and cockroaches, the only animals left alive in large numbers.

To remember what we once had been, people circulated photographs of an enormous oasis with great plantations, parks, and animal sanctuaries full of butterflies and flocks of birds, at the bottom of which was printed, "Come and visit us. The Emirate of Emirs is a paradise."

The first one to attempt it was a good swimmer who took the precaution of carrying food and medicine. Then a whole family left, then whole villages, large and small. The population dropped considerably. One fine day there was nobody left, with the exception of the president and his cabinet. Everyone else, even the deputies, followed the rest by opening the cover of the aqueduct and floating all the way to the cover at the other end, doorway to the Emirate of the Emirs.

In that country we were second-class citizens, something we were already accustomed to. We lived in a ghetto. We got work because we knew about coffee, sugar cane, cotton, fruit trees, and truck gardens. In a short time we were happy and felt as if these things too were ours, or at the very least, that the rain still belonged to us.

A few years passed; the price of oil began to plunge and plunge. The emir asked for a loan, then another, then many; eventually he had to beg and beg for money to service the loans. The story sounds all too familiar. Now the IMF has taken possession of the aqueducts. They have cut off the water because of a default in payments and because the sultan had the bright idea of receiving as a guest of honor a representative of that country that is a neighbor of ours.

Translated by Jo Anne Engelbert

The Dog

Lyzandro Chávez Alfaro

Adriana pulled the rocker out onto the sidewalk. She arranged her flouncy, full-pleated skirt, her starched petticoats, before sitting down. She was breathing in the hot air heavily. The city was thrown into a steamy darkness; sporadic rifle shots rang out. Not far away, the dim light on the corner lit up part of the street. A few dejected-looking people passed under the lamp, wrapped in a halo of danger. The woman gazed up at the sky, fanning herself and stretching out her lace collar so that the air would go down her bust. What she saw was a furnace throwing off steady sparks; a furnace facing down on the world. A choking anguish was murmuring inside Adriana. Even the clothes she wore hurt her. The balmy voice of the last customer to leave her restaurant interrupted her thoughts:

"Until tomorrow."

"Until tomorrow, and be careful. It's almost curfew time."

"A quarter to eight," the man said looking at his pocket watch. "Have you heard anything about Barcino?" he asked as he pulled a cigar out of his pocket.

"Look, I prefer not to talk about that rotten little animal because . . . because it leaves a bitter taste in my mouth."

Adriana fanned herself using rapid motions and turned her head toward the dark lot that was opposite her house. A deep crack appeared on her forehead. The constant creaking of the rocker filled the silent emptiness of the street. The man lit his cigar, looking out of the corner of his eye at the same time. In the shade, with her plump body filling the rocker and with her ankle boots crossed over one another, she looked like a big seal in clothes. *She gets upset over next to nothing,* he thought, taking a first step.

"Have a good night."

Adriana didn't answer. Barcino, the dog she'd fed for five years of her life, was filling her brain. The unsuspected flight of the animal was beyond her comprehension. She had seen it born in the middle of the street, right in front of her house. His mother, a very deformed she-wolf, weary from having given birth to fifty thousand pups; his father, a robust mastiff with huge, strong paws, pointed ears, and white hair with reddish spots. She had always wanted to have a dog from good roots. "Can I take care of one when they are born?" she used to ask her neighbor. She swore at him again, filled with more hatred.

The echo of the curse conjured up the image of Barcino lying down beside the rocker, with his head between his paws, keeping an eye on everyone who approached. She saw his tail wagging when she fed him cooked meat in the corner of the kitchen; she heard his fierce barking at all hours of the night filling her house, making her feel safe. All the little things—

the way his jowls moved when he barked, the helpless trembling all over his body after every bath, the humility with which he listened when she scolded him, the whiteness of his teeth, the sound of his nails on the tile floor, the gleam of his tongue hanging out when he returned from the streets—forming the skin and bones of Adriana's drama.

Some light steps echoed behind her. She stopped rocking and fanning herself, and without turning around, she fixed her attention behind her back. The steps were coming closer, and Adriana was piecing together the figure of her neighbor.

"What? Are you crazy to be sitting here, at this hour and during these times!" the neighbor said, placing her basket in her other hand.

"What more can happen! That one of their bullets kills me? If they would only do me the favor!"

"Don't talk like that, Adriana." She began to moan, gazing into the empty basket. "What will they do to my poor husband. I was waiting two hours in the yard of the barracks, and they didn't let me see him. Maybe they didn't give him the clothes and food that I brought. You have no idea how those *pigs* treat you. It's horrible! They're going to kill him, and it wasn't him, it wasn't him!"

"How do you know?" Adriana scratched her neck with the fan and contracted her face. "I'd not only poison their water; I'd poison the air they breathe if I could."

There was a pause in which both were plunged into their own anguish. The neighbor wiped her nose on her arm before resuming the conversation:

"You have no idea who I saw in the barracks. He was looking so proud, like he was right at home . . ." Adriana let out an empty sound, still wrapped up within herself. "I was sitting on a bench, waiting, when

I saw him crossing the yard behind a *pig* . . ." Adriana stopped fanning herself and abruptly sat up straight, grasping the arms of the rocker. The words *I saw him* made her back stiffen. She knew whom she had seen. Two days ago she learned the whereabouts of her dog, but feeling ashamed to show how she had been abandoned by the one she loved most, she tried to hide it as much as she could. "'Is it him?' I asked myself. But you couldn't mistake him. In all of Granada there isn't another like him. 'Barcino!' I shouted at him, and he just turned around and looked at me with an air of contempt, I swear."

Adriana grew tense, she held her breath, her nostrils opened wide, flaring up, her whole face turned flush— until she could no longer bear the weight of her shoulders and had to breathe out before she burst. She stared into the darkness and spoke in a faltering voice, her eyes blinking from nervousness:

"These things happen, and one doesn't believe it until it does happen . . . because there's poison everywhere . . . ingratitude . . . what ingratitude! Shameless even for animals! And I'm not saying that only my dog is capable of such treachery. I have seen men and women laughing with the filibusters with the same lack of scruples. If not, tell me who are the ones who serve them and even entertain them in their houses. . . . And my dog . . . no! He isn't my dog! I have nothing to do with him, and I never want to have anything to do with him again. . . . Who knows if animals learn from people or if they learn from animals. . . . Why did he do it? For a piece of ham, a half-rotten apple, or even for a look from their pretty blue eyes. . . . I didn't want to believe it. No, no. But I went to spy on the barracks, and it was exactly what they had told me. I think he even has a different bark now. . . . They gave him an English name, and he's as meek as a lamb and comes every time they call his name. You should see him! How he wags his tail and laps it all up, swooning. . . . I loved him . . . Even if he had gone hungry with me, but you saw how he ate. Even if I was hitting him, but when did I ever hit him for no reason. . . . And even if all that had been so, he didn't have any right to go off with the first *pig* who winked at him. . . . What's really going on is that—"

The bugle resounded over the rooftops, contracting and extending the curfew into sorrow-stricken corners. Doors were closing, lights were going out, conversations were being cut short. By the time the bugle call had ended, Granada almost stopped breathing, possessed by a vague premonition of its ruin, reduced to rubble. "Good night," the neighbor mumbled.

Adriana continued rocking and fanning herself as though unperturbed, but without showing her face. She heard a last sound of doors closing and then a deep silence that covered everything, like a mosquito net over someone sick. Some distant barks caused her to close her eyes and grimace in disgust, imagining Barcino beside the bed of the filibuster. "Watkins, it is Captain Watkins," they had told her when she asked who was the dog's new, adopted friend.

Two shots rang out in the night. Rather than let herself feel afraid of getting hit by a bullet, she tried to dissolve into the darkness. She didn't move. She leaned her head back and gazed up. Torn curtains began to fall from the sky, or over her cloudy eyes. Barcino leaped among them, barking and horribly happy. "The American Falange" was marching down the road. *No. I don't want to see them. What am I going to buy tomorrow at the market? With the shortages* . . . But the mercenaries recruited in New Orleans, Charleston or Mobile continued to march under the morning sun in their pretentious uniforms. Banners were waving above the stages erected in the plaza. *Such silence. When I go to the cemetery I get the chills.* Mariano Salazar was dressing his wounds himself. "To arms!" he yelled in a loud, bitter yet firm voice. *Long live Salazar!* she thought of shouting. *They're going to say that I'm crazy.* The banners were waving, and the stage collapsed along with him. His chest had been crushed. The banners were barking. Barcino was waving, showing his black fangs. The feeble voice of William Walker drifted out over the heads of the spectators gathered in the plaza. *Why do I have to listen to him!* She covered her ears with her hands. The waves from the lake roared without muffling his voice. Speaking in English, he accepted the duties as President of Nicaragua. *To think that he came barely a year ago, in the service of the "democrats." And now they are the "legitimate" ones who are in the saddle. Please explain that to me! No . . . screw them!* Up on the stage, Fermin Ferrer thanked the Almighty for having sent Walker to Nicaragua. The cannon salutes, the applause of Ambassador Wheeler and Father Vigil—as black as his cassock—the barks of Barcino, rarified the air. With a great effort she left that dislocated mental state. *It is the 2nd of August, 1856. The second of August, 1856. The second of August,* she repeated desperately. She wanted to hold onto the date as onto a life jacket. But the current was stronger than she. Again she heard the dog barking in the street amidst the sound of the drums. She would've liked to have him inside her house, hitting him until his ribs cracked. *Do you really think slavery will return?* she had asked one of her customers. *I'm certain. You have to read between the lines. Did you read Walker's decree? Well, if all the prior decrees are repealed, then the one abolishing slavery also is abolished.* A shooting star fell across the sky and saved her from sure disaster. *They jump around like fleas*, she mumbled, expressing her personal bitterness.

The night patrol made up of five soldiers from the Falange formed on the street corner. Adriana slowly rocked with defiant deliberateness. They were walking casually, in no rush, each one holding his rifle in the most comfortable way. The woman just waited in silence, hurling stones at them in her mind: *Look at those faces. They can't disguise what they are—bandits! If only I were a burning ray. Those eyes! If only I were a vulture . . . I swear I wouldn't touch them.*

One of the soldiers came forward. He stopped next to her and pointed inside the house with his rifle.

"Get in and close your door. Right now!"

"I don't understand anything. Leave me alone."

"Oh, come on; in there!" the soldier yelled, lifting her up out of the rocker in one motion. Adriana entered her house wiping off her arm. Behind her, they kicked over the rocker and uttered several phrases that she just knew were filthy.

Guns, bottles and laughter echoed throughout the barracks of the Falange. The Nicaraguans had awakened on the brink of slavery, and they were prepared to defend themselves. William Walker's soldiers were getting ready to go and destroy the band that had seized a hacienda where they were stocking up on meat.

Sitting on his bed, Captain Watkins was carefully tying up his leather leggings. Beside him, Barcino raised his head. He was watching his new friend with a hunger to serve, overwhelmed by the strange odor that emanated from the armpits of the foreigner. He admired him, and licking his chops, he seemed to say: Watkins, Watkins, how strong you are! The captain smiled, gave him a little tap on his snout and said something to him that he took as a compliment. Watkins stood up, hitting his leggings several times to test them, and went over to the washbasin. The animal took a few steps in the same direction, moving his back in an exaggerated manner. He was imitating the ungainly walk of the officer. When Watkins finished washing his face, he uttered something that only the dog could understand and snapped his fingers. With a leap, Barcino grabbed the towel between his teeth and placed it in the hands of his friend.

"Okay, Ranger. Ready to fight? That's a good boy."

Ranger answered with a mean growl. Watkins combed his hair before a mirror that was hanging on the wall; the dog continued watching his every movement, with all his muscles taught and his tongue hanging out. He guessed that it was time to leave. Before his friend would finish strapping on his sword and pistol, the dog was at the door in two leaps.

In the yard, the gathered soldiers were cleaning the barrels of their rifles, adjusting the gunsights, filling their canteens with water, arranging their knapsacks or simply chewing tobacco.

"Ranger, Ranger!" someone called out. The dog ran to the center of the yard. Laughing amongst themselves, the soldiers gave him slaps on the ass and pulled on his ears. His eyes were dancing, and with his tail he was repeating: We are friends, good friends! We are friends, good friends!

At dusk, the column of filibusters left the city. The slanted rays of the sun stretched over the road, casting a file of gigantic shadows. Ranger projected a shadow that looked like the silhouette of a rhinoceros. He was walking up ahead, stopping in places in order to sniff the grass that curiously grew in the little ruts. One of the soldiers started singing a popular song from the South of the United States. In no time the entire body of troops was singing in chorus. Excited by the song, the dog started doing pirouettes, barking, hurling himself ferociously at the branches moving in the wind, biting his tail and running around like a mad dog, describing elipses around the column. Darkness settled in. The troops didn't stop singing, and the dog didn't stop jumping about all over the place. How lucky to be part of that powerful force!

The early morning light fell over a plain, sparkling with dew, in the middle of which was a big stone house. The filibusters organized themselves into three flanks for the attack. The bugle sounded strange calls, over and over again, resounding over the shooting and chasing a flock of little clouds toward the objective. Ranger advanced without leaving his boss's side, until he could see close-up the barricades that surrounded the house. The three flanks were repelled one after the other. They regrouped and again launched the attack. The flank that Watkins commanded penetrated one of their barricades and plunged into hand-to-hand combat. Now the dog could demonstrate his bravery and loyalty. He would aim for the shoulders of each Nicaraguan fighter that the captain attacked with his sword, and in one leap sink his teeth into the fighter's neck. The smell of gunpowder, the clamor of the combatants, the brackish taste of blood, filled his glands with an ancestral ferocity that frightened even his boss for a moment. In the most intense moment of the fighting, a bayonet ripped open Watkins' belly. He fell on his back and a bluish bubbly ooze, streaked with fat and blood, flowed from the wound. The animal covered him with his body; he growled and bared his teeth at the shadows that were moving through the cloud of dust and smoke that enveloped them. Transformed into some fiery mythological monster, there he was with his seven heads and his wings of iron protecting his fallen friend.

They heard the pounding of hundreds of hoofbeats on the plain, and the filibusters sounded the retreat. There was barely time to carry off the wounded, first as bloody bundles, and, later, on improvised stretchers.

Watkins was groaning in pain; his eyes were closed, and his legs and arms were totally limp, while the unrelenting sun burned his intestines. The dispersed column crossed an open Nicaraguan plain. The earth rose up in clouds of dust that got into the eyes, nostrils, wounds, and caused the dying Watkins to groan in pain. The dog was walking along in the shadows of the stretchers. His head was raised, his muscles soft, limp, weary from grief. The captain was making gurgling sounds in his throat. He was delirious, mumbling promises, pleading for peace for his belly, for his oozing blood, but the two men who were carrying him were more preoccupied with their parched lips, and even more with their unexpected defeat.

When the groans of the dying man became constant, the commander ordered that they stop under a ceiba tree. They gave him water and tried to revive him. Sweat was pouring off him, and they just looked at him, furious at those responsible for Watkins' condition. Ranger slipped between the legs of those who were standing around his friend, and in a desperate act, he wanted to lick his intestines. Before he could anoint his tongue on the oozing pile, a flurry of kicks covered him from his snout to his tail. A yelp that he couldn't get out made his teeth chatter as he fled, nearly crawling. Amidst the whirl of insults by some of the soldiers, a rifle came flying at him with its bayonet fixed. Even with his quick movements, he was barely able to escape. The rifle landed and stuck in the ground right between his paws.

Hidden among the bushes by the side of the road, he watched Watkins being buried. The low whispers of a prayer and then the clear "Amen" flew up through the trees. When they started to march again, Ranger went up to the grave. He sniffed the mound of earth, the cross made out of two branches. A deep, trembling howl resonated in his bones, and he pawed at the grave for a moment. With his dirty snout, he sniffed about the whole area. He was alone. He sprang out into the road and saw in the distance a black speck with silvery sparkles. He ran toward it, but, on seeing the soldiers up close, he turned to slip away among the bushes. So, keeping a safe distance, he entered Granada with them. The people watched them march by, filthy, weary, and they sneered at them in disgust.

"Guess what? I saw Barcino in the street today. He was all bones and filthy. I guess he's no longer in the barracks of the Falange," one of the restaurant customers said, as he stirred his soup with the spoon.

"Oh, really?" Adriana commented matter-of-factly, and continued folding the tablecloths.

A carriage passed by, and a pack of dogs started barking at the horses. Adriana looked out the door without giving it a second thought. Watching the coachman who was cracking his whip on both sides of the coach, she knew she was waiting for Barcino. It was a wait filled with a mixture of compassion and hatred, of disgust and affection. A painful repugnance welled up inside her, together with the desire to seize the whip and lash that pack of dogs until they were cut to pieces. She felt her hands sweating, and she wiped them on her apron. "I don't think he has the nerve to show up here," she said and returned to her work.

Two days passed. The next morning, as she was combing her hair, she went out to open the door. The bells of a church clock were ringing the time: five o'clock. Barcino was sitting on the sidewalk. When he saw her, he bolted out into the middle of the street, with his tail between his legs and his ears lowered. The surprise paralyzed her. Her first impulse was to pick up a club and fling it at the dog with all the force of her anger, but she contained herself. With her mouth gaping and the comb in her hand, she looked up and down the street; there was no one.

"Don't just sit there looking silly. If you're coming in, come on in," she said in a calm voice, as she finished combing her hair with seeming indifference.

The dog moved one ear, but he didn't dare take a step forward. He was figuring out up to what point he could trust the apparent calmness of the woman.

"He thinks I'm going to whip him, because he's got it coming. . . . Come on in, sonofabitch!" she said under her breath, putting on a friendly face and turning to go inside.

In the kitchen, the cook and a boy were having breakfast.

"Good morning. How do you feel today?"

Adriana didn't respond. She served herself coffee with warm milk and sat down next to the stove. In the yard the birds were making a racket just like every day. But apart from that, it was quiet and rather solemn.

"Look who's here!" the boy yelled out when he saw the head of the dog appear in the kitchen doorway.

"But there's no reason to shout, silly boy," Adriana said, her lips coated with milk. "Tie him up in the yard and give him something to eat."

Barcino allowed himself to be tied up without putting up the least resistance. He ate like he was dying of starvation. When Adriana came out, he licked his

snout and wagged his tail, celebrating the reconciliation. The woman, with her arms crossed, maintained
her offended attitude. She remembered when he was a
month old, the red ribbon bow adorning his collar.
Through the tears in her eyes, she tried to look at the
branches of the tamarind tree whose shadow covered
half the yard. She wiped her nose with one hand and
took out some money from her apron pocket with the
other.

"Go rent a burro. And buy twenty yards of rope; the
heaviest you see."

"A burro and rope?" the boy questioned, not sure
whether to take the money.

"Yes! Go do what I tell you, quickly, and don't ask
questions about what doesn't concern you!" Adriana
yelled, drowning in tears.

The dog barked in the same tone as in the days
when Adriana lived for him. He yanked on the leash in
his desire to be close to her. "No, it's too late to make
peace," she mumbled and left him to bark. She contem-
plated the tree, with that quiet unrest of one who sees a
storm approaching. The birds had fled. She cut off a
branch from a lemon tree. She sat down on a rock and
slowly started pulling off the leaves. One question kept
hammering in her head: Why did he do it? Why did
he do it? Why did he do it? Whatever answer she
found only served to reaffirm her decision. A dark
wind filled the yard, where everything had been infected with the severity of her sentence. Between each
leaf, she glanced over towards the door.

"You kill a snake, and this swine is full of deadly
poison," she said, and went to meet the boy who had
just entered mounted on a burro. Very calmly she took
the rope and tested its strength. She threw it over a
high limb of the tamarind tree. She made a slipknot on
one end and tied the other end around the burro's

neck. She acted with precision, as if she had rehearsed what she was doing for months. With two agile movements, she slipped the knot around Barcino's neck. The dog began shivering, silent, his tail curled under. He was shaking his head, gyrating in circles, seeking mercy in the eyes of the woman. She looked at him with something more than the rage of a woman toward her unfaithful husband. Hitting him on his shoulder with the stick, she pulled him over next to the burro.

"There will be plenty of those who curse me and call me perverse, wicked, and who knows how many things . . . but justice is justice," she said, as though confessing to the yard. "Gee up, burro!"

The crack of the blow that Adriana put to the buttocks of the beast resounded for several blocks around. The whole tree shook. The dog, with its white tongue and red teeth, was left there swaying.

Translated by Richard Schaaf

Boardinghouse

Claribel Alegría

On December 23, 1972, Francisco Ramírez trudged despairingly through the hot, dusty streets of Managua in search of a hotel room. All were filled. With parched throat and a suitcase that weighed more with each step, he turned aside and entered a bar just off the main street. Though it was nearly 5 P.M., this bar was almost empty. He set the suitcase down beside a corner table, sank wearily into a chair and signaled the waiter.

"A cold beer, please."

He wished it were already tomorrow, reunited with his wife and children and making preparations for Christmas Eve. His plane would leave at 9 A.M. A few more hours.

He sipped his beer slowly, visualizing Rosario's and Paquito's faces as they opened the boxes containing the doll that pees and an astronaut in a space suit. He smiled to himself and gazed about the room.

Another solitary drinker at one of the center tables raised his bottle in salutation. Francisco nodded in reply. A minute later the other was standing beside his table, holding the bottle and a glass.

"May I?"

"Of course."

What a drag, Francisco thought to himself, *but what can I do? That's the way these nicas are.*

"Fernando Silva," the other introduced himself.

"Francisco Ramírez."

"Are you leaving or arriving?" the other asked as he sat down.

"Both. I arrived this afternoon from Costa Rica, and I'm leaving tomorrow morning for El Salvador. I've spent the past two hours hunting for a hotel room, but there aren't any."

"It's difficult this time of year."

They chatted about the Managua heat now that the rainy season had ended, about the collapse of the Central American Common Market since the Football War three years before, about the beautiful tica women. Silva did most of the talking.

"It's almost six-thirty," Francisco emptied the last of his fourth beer. "Do you happen to know where I could find a hotel or a boardinghouse?"

"As a matter of fact I do," the other's face lit up. "A friend of mine, Benedicto Aguilar, owns a small hotel not too far from here. Tell him I recommended you. From the corner," he gestured, "it's three blocks toward the lake and one block west. Hotel Villavicencio. Number forty-seven."

"You've saved my life," Francisco said warmly. "Thanks very much." He gestured to the waiter.

"No, no, please," Silva stopped him. "You're my guest."

They said good-bye, exchanging pats on the shoulder like old friends.

172

Francisco set the suitcase down, exhaled gustily, and mopped his face with his handkerchief before ringing the bell. A woman dressed in a pink uniform opened the door.

"Yes?"

"Is Señor Aguilar in?"

"Who shall I say is calling?"

"He doesn't know me, but a friend of his sent me here. A Fernando Silva."

"Come in and sit down," the woman said. "I'll call him." She closed the door behind him and disappeared.

Francisco lowered the suitcase to the floor and sat down in one of the two easy chairs upholstered in red plastic. The entrance was small and seemed over-crowded with the single sofa, two chairs, center table, magazine stand and two potted ferns. Behind it was the reception desk with a telephone and against the wall a board from which dangled numbered room keys. He observed that none of the keys was missing. Strange, he thought. Could I be the only guest?

"Good afternoon," the owner appeared. Francisco arose and shook hands with him.

"Please sit down."

"I accidentally ran into a friend of yours, Fernando Silva, and he told me that you might have a room available."

That idiot! Aguilar told himself. *Another of his practical jokes.*

"I'm sorry," he told the stranger, "but I'm afraid we haven't any empty rooms." A woman, dressed in black skirt and white, short-sleeved blouse, slid behind the reception desk. Francisco glanced at her and, startled, stared again.

"Matilde," Aguilar addressed her, "we don't have any vacancies, do we?"

"Not a one," she replied.

"What terrible luck," Francisco said. "Could you let me spend the night on that sofa or in any odd corner if you have a cot? All the hotels are filled, and I'm leaving for El Salvador in the morning."

"I'm sorry, but that won't be possible," Aguilar shook his head. "But while I try to think how I can help you, won't you join me in a drink?" He addressed Matilde again. "Put his suitcase behind the reception desk." As he ushered Francisco down the hallway and into the small bar, he explained, "We have to be especially careful about sneak thieves this time of year. Where would you like to sit? Here, or beside the window?"

"It makes no difference," Francisco replied.

There was no one else in the room, and they sat at one of the four tables. Francisco observed that a bottle of rum and a half-empty glass stood on the table near the window. A row of bottles lined the shelf behind the bar, and perched atop the grandfather clock in the corner, a stuffed black crow opened its wings.

A woman bearing an extraordinary resemblance to the others glided into the room wearing a white organdy apron and a coif. They must all be sisters, Francisco decided.

"Two Extra Secos, Rosita," Aguilar told her. Then, turning to Francisco, "How will you have yours?"

"With ice and a little water."

"A few drops of lemon?"

"That would be fine."

"So Silva recommended my hotel, did he?"

"That's right."

Aguilar shook his head reprovingly.

"He knows very well that all my guests are permanent and I never have extra rooms."

"It looks very comfortable," Francisco wheedled. "Are you sure you can't find a corner for me upstairs?"

"It was never meant to be a hotel in the first place," Aguilar ignored his question. "My grandfather, who came from Matagalpa, bought the old part of the house, which was set back from the street, and he started enlarging it to accommodate members of the family when they came to Managua."

Rosita silently served their two rums and set a plate of dried shrimp between them.

"All this front part and the second floor were built by my grandfather."

"You must come from a large family."

"Yes. The old man had eight grown children when he arrived here, and he wanted to be able to accommodate the whole tribe."

"This is excellent rum," Francisco said. "I like it better than the Cuban. Could you tell me where the toilets are?"

"At the end of the hall, to the right."

When he returned, he noticed that Aguilar's glass was almost empty.

"What happened was that all his children except my father preferred living in Matagalpa," Aguilar continued as if there had been no interruption. "They're all dead now, and we grandchildren are scattered all over Central America and the United States."

Francisco heard him out patiently, nibbling at the shrimp and sipping his rum slowly.

"My father left the house to me when he died." Aguilar turned to the bar. "Rosita, bring us two more rums. Better yet, bring the bottle and some ice cubes so we don't have to keep bothering you."

"No, no," Francisco raised a hand. "This is plenty for me."

"But we have the whole night ahead of us," Aguilar protested.

Francisco exhaled contentedly. That meant he would sleep here.

"Ask Juana what's on the menu," Aguilar told Rosita when she brought them the bottle and ice bucket.

"Do you live alone here?" Francisco asked.

"That's right. My wife died five years ago, and we had no children."

There was an uncomfortable pause.

"Fortunately, I also inherited a good library, and I distract myself playing chess with my friends. Do you play?"

"Very badly."

The kitchen door half opened, and a woman in a gray smock peered around it. She was amazingly similar to all the others.

"All we have tonight is breaded shrimp or Jalapeño filet," she announced from the doorway.

"You'll have to forgive us," Aguilar apologized. "As I told you, it's a family hotel."

"Not at all," Francisco assured him. "Jalapeño filet is one of my favorite dishes."

"I'll have the shrimp," Aguilar decided. "And tell Matilde to take the gentleman's suitcase to the old lady's room."

"You don't know how much I appreciate this," Francisco exclaimed. "I was beginning to think I'd have to sleep in the park."

"You're lucky," Aguilar told him. "The woman who has the room went to Estelí to spend the holidays with her family. Ordinarily, I wouldn't have done this, but I feel I can trust you."

"Thanks very much," Francisco said earnestly.

"I warn you, it's not the best room you've ever seen. It's in the old part of the house near the kitchen, but it has a bathroom. All the others are in the new part."

"How many are there?"

"Seven, all told. I occupy the bridal suite and have my library there. I'll show you the books. I have all of Jules Verne. Do you like his work?"

"Of course."

"All of Humboldt's voyages. They were my grand-father's. I also have almost all of Edgar Allan Poe. I'm a great fan of his. That bird up there," he pointed to the clock, "is named Edgar in his honor. Do you like Poe?"

"I know only a few of his short stories."

"'Quoth the raven, Nevermore,'" Aguilar recited in deplorable English. "It's a shame we don't get more books here. El Salvador must be the same, no?"

"That's right. There's only one halfway decent book-store."

"This is the Third World, my friend. Will you have another rum?"

"Not yet," Francisco shook his head. "I'm fine."

"But for me, there's no one like Carlos Castaneda," Aguilar poured himself another drink. "Have you read him?"

"No. I've heard his name mentioned."

"I swear that his tales about Don Juan changed my life."

"Why is that?" Francisco asked attentively.

"I wouldn't know how to explain it. You'll have to read him for yourself. He takes you into another world that was right here all the time, only you weren't able to see it. If you can't find his books in El Salvador, order them from Mexico. I've never read anything that im-pressed me so much, not even the Bible."

"I'll look for it when I get home," Francisco prom-ised. "Perhaps my wife knows of him, she's more of a reader than I am. With my work in the bank, I don't have time to read anything but economics."

Aguilar downed three more rums as they chatted, while Francisco limited himself to a single one. Even-tually, Matilde appeared and announced, "Your room is ready, sir. Would you like me to show you to it?"

"Yes," Francisco stood up gratefully. "I'd like to take a shower before dinner."

"Go right ahead," Aguilar said jovially. "We'll call you when Juana is ready to serve."

As Francisco stepped out into the hallway, Matilde turned and glared at Aguilar.

"You'll be sorry," she hissed. She turned abruptly and left the room. Francisco followed her down the hall, observing her figure carefully. The same slender waist and strong hips. Even the same shoes! Could it be?

She opened the door and handed him his key.

"I hope you'll be comfortable," she said and left.

The room was small, its walls covered with a flowered paper. The furnishings were austere: a single bed, a night table, a desk, chair and a wardrobe that was locked. Not a single picture or even a calendar. Nothing to indicate that anyone lived here. He thrust his head out the single window that gave onto the back patio. Two cats slunk around a garbage can. The sky was partly covered with heavy black clouds, and a reddish moon was half visible. *This place is an inferno*, he told himself. *I've never felt so hot in my life*. And not a breath of air.

What an idiot I am, Aguilar said to himself as he slowly sipped his rum. *I've broken the rules of the game, and that's serious.*

His thick body slumped in the chair and he passed a hand over his face. *I've been a fool, and they're all furious with me.* As if to confirm his thought, Juana stalked out of the kitchen, took the bottle off the table, and placed it behind the bar.

"You've had enough," she said abruptly, and she returned to the kitchen.

What's done is done, Aguilar thought glumly, staring

down at the remaining liquid in his glass. *Don't let anything happen to us, little Virgin. I swear I'll never do it again.* He raised his glass, and his gaze passed over the other tables.

"Cheers," he said aloud, "and please forgive me, all of you."

Francisco felt refreshed after his shower. From his suitcase he selected the yellow *guayabera* that Lupe liked, stuffed his soggy shirt into a plastic bag and closed the lid. He turned off the light, thinking it might cool the room, and lay down on the bed without removing the flowered spread.

Everything in this hotel is strange, starting with the quadruplets. Surely they must be quadruplets. Lupe would have already found out. She'll be happy with her perfume, he smiled up into the darkness. *I hope Aguilar doesn't keep gabbing at me all night. He's another strange one; must be an alcoholic. Ah, Lupe, Lupe. A few hours more and I'll be with you and the kids. These trips are harder to take all the time. You won't believe me when I tell you I didn't so much as go to a movie. Could it be old age? They say baldness isn't a sign of old age, but lack of enthusiasm is.*

"Dinner is ready," Rosita announced, approaching Aguilar's table.

"Very well," Aguilar told her. "Go and knock on our guest's door. And Rosita—what do you think of my mistake?"

"I don't like it a bit," her voice was curt, "but you're the boss."

"I know. I'm a fool. Go tell him dinner is ready."

The dining room table was long and narrow. It was set for ten people.

"Hasn't anyone else arrived?" Francisco asked as he sat down across from Aguilar.

"No. With the holidays, everybody stays out late," Aguilar's voice was thick and blurred. "Nobody else is going to eat here, so help yourself. Rosita! Bring us two cold beers."

"Tell me something," Francisco said as he served himself the filet, "are the girls quadruplets?"

"They look alike, don't they?" Aguilar smiled. "Here, have some rice. How did you like your room?"

"Just fine."

"I'll have Matilde bring you a fan. It's terribly hot tonight. Most unusual for December. It's hotter here than in San Salvador, isn't it?"

"Much, much hotter," Francisco replied. He was already perspiring again.

"Well, you needn't exaggerate," Aguilar said stiffly.

He's dead drunk, Francisco thought.

"How about a game of chess?" Aguilar asked when they finished eating.

"No, thanks. If you don't mind, I'd really rather turn in now. It's been a very tough day."

"As you please." Aguilar glanced at his watch. "It's not even ten o'clock yet. What time do you want us to wake you?"

"Don't bother. I have an alarm clock. Will it be easy to catch a cab to the airport? I have to be there at seven."

"No trouble. Rosita will call you one. Have a good night's sleep."

"I'm sleepy myself," Aguilar mumbled as he lurched up the stairway. "Let's leave the match for tomorrow night if that's all right with you, Capablanca."

No sooner had he turned off the light than Aguilar felt a sharp earth tremor. He sat up, switched on the light again, put on his bedroom slippers and waited, sitting on the edge of the bed.

Two hours later, the world fell apart with a sickening jolt, and Aguilar awakened in bedlam. His wardrobe crashed to the floor. Outside in the street people were screaming and shouting. The room was suddenly filled with dust, and he was sneezing as he groped for the light switch. He switched it on and off several times. No electricity. He pulled on his pants, got into bedroom slippers and groped his way around the fallen wardrobe. The door was jammed, and he jerked at the knob desperately until it creaked open. The screams and moans from the street were growing worse.

"Benedicto, Benedicto," someone called from the hallway.

"Lolita, is that you?" She was holding a flashlight.

"Who else, *tonto*? Don't you see my bathrobe?"

"It's a terrible quake. We have to get out of here."

They embraced each other, trembling, and she lighted the way down the sagging stairway past a fissure that had opened in the wall. In the vestibule, the chandelier and the plants were on the floor. Lolita shone her light toward the back of the house, illuminating a pile of rubble and broken tiles where the old section had collapsed.

"Our visitor!" Aguilar clutched his head in both hands. "Señor Ramírez! Señor Ramírez!" he bellowed. "Can you hear me?"

There was no reply.

"It's your fault," she snapped at him. "I told you you'd be sorry. Now let's get out of here before an aftershock brings the whole place down.

Aguilar stumbled behind her, dazed, into the chaos of the street. Clouds of dust swirled about them. Flashlights and candles moved here and there. Naked children ran about, screaming for their mothers. Some of the ghostlike figures were draped in sheets, and tongues of flame started licking up from the rubbled remains of houses, offering an eerie, flickering illumination. Screams and moans came from some of the ruins.

"Let's head for the park before somebody grabs our flashlight," Lolita took Aguilar by the arm and commenced tugging him through the broken tiles and crumbled masonry that littered the street, carefully avoiding dangling power cables.

"Inocencio's room, Lolita."

She stopped and stared at him.

"Have you lost your mind?"

"Inocencio's room," Aguilar insisted, gripping her elbow fiercely. "We'll make Inocencio's room ready for him. It's the least I can do to make up for what I've done."

Translated by Darwin J. Flakoll

Mister Taylor

Augusto Monterroso

 "Somewhat less strange, although surely more exemplary," the other man said then, "is the story of Mr. Percy Taylor, a headhunter in the Amazon jungle.

"In 1937 he is known to have left Boston, Massachusetts, where he had refined his spirit to the point at which he did not have a cent. In 1944 he appears for the first time in South America, in the region of the Amazon, living with the Indians of a tribe whose name there is no need to recall.

"Because of the shadows under his eyes and his famished appearance, he soon became known as 'the poor gringo,' and the school children even pointed at him and threw stones when he walked by, his beard shining in the golden tropical sun. But this caused no distress to Mr. Taylor's humble nature, for he had read in the first volume of William C. Knight's *Complete Works* that poverty is no disgrace if one does not envy the wealthy.

"In a few weeks the natives grew accustomed to him and his eccentric clothing. Besides, since he had blue eyes and a vague foreign accent, even the president and the minister of foreign affairs treated him with singular respect, fearful of provoking international incidents.

"He was so wretchedly poor that one day he went into the jungle to search for plants to eat. He had walked several meters without daring to turn his head when, by sheerest accident, he saw a pair of Indian eyes observing him intently from the undergrowth. A long shudder traveled down Mr. Taylor's sensitive spine. But Mr. Taylor intrepidly defied all danger and continued on his way, whistling as if he had not seen anything.

"With a leap, which there is no need to call feline, the native landed in front of him and cried: 'Buy head? Money, money.'

"Although the Indian's English could not have been worse, Mr. Taylor, feeling somewhat ill, realized the Indian was offering to sell him an oddly shrunken human head that he was carrying in his hand.

"It is unnecessary to say that Mr. Taylor was in no position to buy it, but since he pretended not to understand, the Indian felt horribly embarrassed for not speaking good English and gave the head to him as a gift, begging his pardon.

"Mr. Taylor's joy was great as he returned to his hut. That night, lying on his back on the precariously balanced palm mat that was his bed, and interrupted only by the buzzing of the passionate flies that flew around him as they made love obscenely, Mr. Taylor spent a long time contemplating his curious acquisition with delight. He derived the greatest aesthetic pleasure from counting the hairs of the beard and moustache one by one and looking straight into the two half-ironic eyes that seemed to smile at him in gratitude for his deferential behavior.

"A man of immense culture, Mr. Taylor was contemplative by nature, but on this occasion he soon became bored with his philosophical reflections and decided to give the head to his uncle, Mr. Rolston, who lived in New York and who, from earliest childhood, had shown a strong interest in the cultural manifestations of Latin American peoples.

"A few days later, Mr. Taylor's uncle wrote to ask him (not before inquiring after the state of his precious health) to please favor him with five more. Mr. Taylor willingly satisfied Mr. Rolston's desire and—no one knows how—by return mail he 'was very happy to honor your request.' Extremely grateful, Mr. Rolston asked for another ten. Mr. Taylor was 'delighted to be of service.' But when in a month he was asked to send twenty more, Mr. Taylor, simple and bearded but with a refined artistic sensibility, had the presentiment that his mother's brother was making a profit off of the heads.

"And, if you want to know, that's how it was. With complete frankness Mr. Rolston told him about it in an inspired letter whose strictly businesslike terms made the strings of Mr. Taylor's sensitive spirit vibrate as never before.

"They immediately formed a corporation: Mr. Taylor agreed to obtain and ship shrunken heads on a massive scale while Mr. Rolston would sell them as best he could in his country.

"In the early days there were some annoying difficulties with certain local types. But Mr. Taylor, who in Boston had received the highest grades for his essay on Joseph Henry Silliman, proved to be a politician and obtained from the authorities not only the necessary export permit but also an exclusive concession for ninety-nine years. It was not difficult for him to convince the chief executive warrior and the legislative witch doctors that such a patriotic move would shortly enrich the community, and that very soon all the thirsty aborigines would be able to have (whenever they wanted a refreshing pause in the collection of heads) an ice cold soft drink whose magic formula he himself would supply.

"When the members of the cabinet, after a brief but luminous exercise of intellect, became aware of these advantages, their love of country bubbled over, and in three days they issued a decree demanding that the people accelerate the production of shrunken heads.

"A few months later, in Mr. Taylor's country, the heads had gained the popularity we all remember. At first they were the privilege of the wealthiest families, but democracy is democracy, and as no one can deny, in a matter of weeks even schoolteachers could buy them.

"A home without its own shrunken head was thought of as a home that had failed. Soon the collectors appeared, and with them, certain contradictions: owning seventeen heads was considered bad taste, but it was distinguished to have eleven. Heads became so popular that the really elegant people began to lose interest and would only acquire one if it had some peculiarity that saved it from vulgarity. A very rare one with Prussian whiskers, that in life had belonged to a highly decorated general, was presented to the Danfeller Institute, which, in turn, immediately donated three and a half million dollars to further the development of this exciting cultural manifestation of Latin American peoples.

"Meanwhile, the tribe had made so much progress that it now had its own path around the Legislative Palace. On Sundays and Independence Day the members of Congress would ride the bicycles the company had given them along that happy path, clearing their throats, displaying their feathers, laughing very seriously.

"But what did you expect? Not all times are good times. Without warning the first shortage of heads occurred.

"Then the best part began.

"Mere natural deaths were no longer sufficient. The minister of public health, feeling sincere one dark night when the lights were out and he had caressed his wife's breast for a little while just out of courtesy, confessed to her that he thought he was incapable of raising mortality rates to the level that would satisfy the interests of the company. To that she replied he should not worry, that he would see how everything would turn out all right, and that the best thing would be for them to go to sleep.

"To compensate for this administrative deficiency it was indispensable that they take strong measures, and a harsh death penalty was imposed.

"The jurists consulted with one another and raised even the smallest shortcoming to the category of a crime punishable by hanging or the firing squad, depending on the seriousness of the infraction.

"Even simple mistakes became criminal acts. For example: if in ordinary conversation someone carelessly said 'It's very hot,' and later it could be proven, thermometer in hand, that it really was not so hot, that person was charged a small tax and executed on the spot, his head sent on to the company, and, it must be said in all fairness, his trunk and limbs passed on to the bereaved.

"The legislation dealing with disease had wide repercussions and was frequently commented on by the diplomatic corps and the ministries of foreign affairs of friendly powers.

"According to this memorable legislation, the gravely ill were given twenty-four hours to put their papers in order and die, but if in this time they were lucky enough to infect their families, they received as many month-long stays as relatives they had infected. The victims of minor illnesses, and those who simply did not feel well, earned the scorn of the fatherland, and anyone on the street was entitled to spit in their faces. For the first time in history the importance of doctors who cured no one was recognized (there were several candidates for the Nobel Prize among them). Dying became an example of the most exalted patriotism, not only on the national level but on that even more glorious one, the continental.

"With the growth achieved by subsidiary industries (coffin manufacture in particular flourished with the technical assistance of the company) the country entered, as the saying goes, a period of great economic prosperity. This progress was particularly evident in a new little flower-bordered path on which, enveloped in the melancholy of the golden autumnal afternoons, the deputies' wives would stroll, their pretty little heads nodding yes, yes, everything was fine, when some solicitous journalist on the other side of the path would greet them with a smile, tipping his hat.

"I remember in passing that one of these journalists, who on a certain occasion emitted a downpour of a sneeze that he could not explain, was accused of extremism and put against the wall facing the firing squad. Only after his unselfish end did the intellectual establishment recognize that the journalist had one of the fattest heads in the country, but once it was shrunken it looked so good that one could not even notice the difference.

"And Mr. Taylor? By this time he had been designated as special adviser to the constitutional president.

Now, and as an example of what private initiative can accomplish, he was counting his thousands by the thousands; but this made him lose no sleep, for he had read in the last volume of the *Complete Works* of William C. Knight that being a millionaire is no dishonor if one does not scorn the poor.

"I believe that this is the second time that I will say that not all times are good times.

"Given the prosperity of the business, the time came when the only people left in the area were the authorities and their wives and the journalists and their wives. Without much effort Mr. Taylor concluded that the only possible solution was to start a war with the neighboring tribes. Why not? This was progress.

"With the help of a few small cannons, the first tribe was neatly beheaded in just under three months. Mr. Taylor tasted the glory of expanding his domain. Then came the second tribe, then the third, the fourth and the fifth. Progress spread so rapidly that the moment came when, regardless of the efforts of the technicians, it was impossible to find neighboring tribes to make war on.

"It was the beginning of the end.

"The little paths began to languish. Only occasionally could one see a lady taking a stroll or some poet laureate with his book under his arm. The weeds once again overran the two paths, making the way difficult and thorny for the delicate feet of the ladies. Along with the heads the bicycles had thinned out, and the happy optimistic greetings had almost completely disappeared.

"The coffin manufacturer was sadder and more funereal than ever. And everyone felt as if they had awakened from a pleasant dream—one of those wonderful dreams when you find a purse full of gold coins, and you put it under your pillow and go back to sleep, and very early the next day, when you wake up, you look for it and find emptiness.

"Nevertheless, business, painfully, went on as usual. But people were having trouble going to sleep for fear they would wake up exported.

"In Mr. Taylor's country, of course, the demand continued to increase. New substitutes appeared daily, but nobody really believed in them, and everyone demanded the little heads from Latin America.

"It happened during the last crisis. A desperate Mr. Rolston was continually demanding more heads. Although the company's stocks suffered a sharp decline, Mr. Rolston was convinced that his nephew would do something to save the situation.

"The once daily shipments decreased to one a month, and they were sending anything: children's heads, ladies' heads, deputies' heads.

"Suddenly they stopped completely.

"One harsh, gray Friday, home from the stock exchange and still dazed by the shouting of his friends and their lamentable show of panic, Mr. Rolston decided to jump out the window (rather than use a gun— the noise would have terrified him). He had opened a package that had come in the mail and found the shrunken head of Mr. Taylor smiling at him from the distant wild Amazon, with a child's false smile that seemed to say 'I'm sorry, I won't do it again.'"

Translated by Edith Grossman

Self-Defense

Fabián Dobles

One that Magdaleno Pérez tells:

"Well, that's how it was: As usual, nothin new around worth talkin about. Waitin for the frog to sprout hair, like they say. Ain't much you can do about it.

"Ah, you wanted to hear about that business? Wasn't no big deal. You boys know that when a Wheel's a Wheel and don't like being messed with, the one that gives the orders gives the order and that's it, if you get my drift. But the one that takes orders, if it ain't in his name, he don't take the blame. On account of—look, friends, when you're at loose ends, you got to latch on to whatever blows your way. Especially, when what you're doin ain't done deliberate.

"Anyhow, to be honest with you boys, I won't say the deal didn't sit fine with me. By then, I'd been back from Guatemala for months. From Chiquimula. I hired out to the whitey meesters and a bunch of stuttergun-totin *criollos*, and so I had dollars in my kick. Then, before I can turn around, bam, they give me the heave. The revolution was cooked, and I'm out on my butt and broke again. The whole gang of us that risked our hides for Castillo and the banana company weren't no use to them no more. But don't you worry . . . I lived it up good with what I had left over from Chiquimula. The only thing is, glory don't last long—pullin trigger don't pay so hot. And when it's over, you ain't nothin but a bother, a burr in the boot."

The little man's smoky-wax face turned to us again. No, it's not a quality of wickedness, exactly. Those eyes of the Central American who's seen it all can have an expression of innocence, even. An innocence of villains . . . such a thing exists. It's the way Magdaleno Pérez grew up; you might almost say that he suckled his first milk out of pistol barrels and from the smoking teats of machine guns, those bony cows that graze the blood-soaked killing fields of Central America.

"Ah, señor," he goes on, laid back, washing his hands, like Pontius Pilate: "that's how it went for me in Costa Rica when I hooked up with the free-for-all in forty-eight; offers galore and, in the end, piss on you. I'm back here again where I hail from, not knowin where to find my next plate of beans, when out of the blue this Wheel I'm talkin about sends for me. We meet over on the bridge.

"'So, who's the mischief with?' I ask him. But he plays 'possum with me.

"'This Christian's name don't concern us. He's a tall fella, well set up, and goes around all the time carryin a big whip.'

"'Let's see, let's see . . . Nope, can't place him. . . . Figure he'll show?'

"'Forget it. You don't have to worry about that part.' And he lets out a little laugh. 'You'll be up against one of those individuals that thinks he's a lot of man. And punctual as a clock, he is. I happen to know he said he'd be there at three, and he'll be there.'

"'All right, so much the better, then. He'll be askin for it.'

"'And don't go gettin me into a bind, hear, because it'll come out the worse for you, but fast. Get me? I'm not for bein messed with. . . . I'll pay you fifty dollars.'

"How about that! I balked and doubled the ante on him, and my boss here, cause he sits in the driver's seat, hands me this: 'Come off it, man, so much for only one? You took seventy-five from those gringos for the blast in Guatemala, didn't you? And that was big stuff.'

"'My gosh, but what a difference there! We were a whole crew that time. Wholesale ain't the same. And on top of it, this one's a *paisano*; and that hurts, y'know.'

"'What makes you say he is?'

"'Easy to smell, boss, and if you'll excuse me, you're expectin to pay peanuts, sir.' I figure this is a fat cat, and I got my self-respect, whatever you think.

"'So what! Fifty, and done with.'

"'Okay, then, but don't go gettin yourself riled up. Fifty, if that's how you want it.'

"I ended havin to accept. You know how it goes, them that's up there, are up there. And they got that kinda gall.

"'But, hey, wait now, that's only if you put out twenty-five on the spot.'

"And don't think he was willin to, the skinflint. But I stuck to my guns, and he finally got it up.

"The other twenty-five was for after. Know what I mean? Then, he starts layin on the recommendations.

"'Play it clean, eh, Magdaleno. Look sharp. Work fast and take no chances. If you screw up—you hear me—I don't even know who you are. You're on your own.'

"Ah, that señor of mine! Then, he winds up with: 'Besides which, this ain't gonna be the first time nor the last. Right, businessman?' And he slips me the wink.

"He had to rub it in, like you hear. As though I get a bang out of these monkeyshines. In this line, you're just askin for it. Take my word!"

"You're not gonna believe this, the damndest fluke you can imagine . . . it turns out to be Graciliano. Graciliano, my old friend from back when. Nope, I couldn't go through with it. How was this here Christian gonna blow the man away without foulin up his conscience for life? No, señores!

"I picked a good position behind the tree, a big *conacaste*, from where I could spot him for a sure shot. I didn't recognize him at first, and I cocked the revolver. I crouched low and crept around to the other side of the tree. I ticked off the seconds, counted his steps, and when I poked my head out you can guess for what, there I am starin right at him from up close. Graciliano! God only knows, I put away my piece and I'm done with him. I ducked back, and not thinkin twice about it, I acted like I happened to be walkin by, whistlin. Like I was on my way to San Rafael. He recognized me right off. Why shouldn't that *ladino* sonofagun recognize me when we'd been such good buddies.

"'Hey, Magdaleno!' he says to me.

"'Ciliano! A dog's age since we seen each other! Seems like a hundred years, don't it, brother?' I acted like he'd took me unawares. What a surprise runnin into you like this, old man, but what a helluva good surprise! I was on my way here to San Rafael, can you beat that!'

"No two ways about it, sometimes you come out with just the words that hit the bullseye. 'Seems to me like you're a little jumpy. What's up? Somethin wrong?' You see, he kept checkin and checkin his watch, tense, like a horse that's waitin on a rider.

"'Nothin, man.' he answered me. 'Expectin a person here at three sharp.'

"He hardly paid me no mind. Kept eyein the road from one end to the other.

"I said to him, 'Ah, I get it. A lady, is it? Same old Graciliano!' And I give him the wink.

"'Nah, nah, nah! Listen, I don't want to hold you up if you have to be in San Rafael!' he says to me, and I could see I was botherin him.

"'If it ain't got to do with a skirt,'—I stayed on the same track cause once the train gets rollin it has to go someplace. What else?—'seems to me like the person ain't gonna show. Certainly seems that way to me. But, I'm sure glad I got to run into you!'

"And, well, I give him the big hug a couple times while he keeps on not payin me no mind. He was off on his own kick all right, and I knew it, but guys, I had to get out of the bind I'd put myself in and cover myself on the job I was hired for.

"'Packin a weapon, eh, Graciliano?'

"'Yeah, maybe so. You never know . . . just in case, pal.'

"'I get you. But, man, never mind that. I'm gettin an idea. . . . Yep, you're just the one I was lookin for. I closed a nice little deal today, and there's nothin I'd like better than to celebrate with you. So, why don't you come on to San Rafael with me? We'll have ourselves a good long talk and tie one on. What a long time it's been, brother!'

"Graciliano kept lookin from one side to the other, whappin away all the while at a big root of that tree with his whip.

"'I guarantee he won't show. You'll see,' I told him and put my hand on his shoulder again. He brushed it off like a horsefly had lit on him.

"'If you want to go, then go. I'm busy. Say . . .!' And all of sudden he turns and looks at me. 'What the hell do you know about this?'

"'Aw, come on, I was only sayin I wanted we should celebrate this little deal together. A person decides to do somethin and then he don't do it. It gets fouled up, on account of there's just no way. And that's all.'

"'What in the hell are you talkin about?'

"'Nothin, man, only beatin my gums. Pay me no mind. It's just that we got so much ground to cover. How's about we really tie on a snootful?' I insisted with him. 'Just forget about this person that didn't show. . . . Who knows, maybe it's better he shouldn't make it? Could be. I don't know.'

"Graciliano looked at his watch. Another few minutes had gone by.

"'I got a wad I wanna get rid of that's beginnin to stink up my pocket,' I kept on tellin him. 'Let's go, pal. Maybe I'll be keepin you outa trouble.'

"What a pigheaded man, that Graciliano! He still had to think it over.

"'Make up your mind, brother. Come with your guardian angel.'

"Finally, he decided he'd go along. On the road, jawin away the both of us, I'd sneak a look at him every once in a while. I couldn't have told you if he was glad he came or if he was teed off at me. A little of each, I reckon. A man straight as him didn't maybe feel just right walkin away from the *conacaste*, but he was there right on the dot, that's for sure. As far as I go, I can tell you I felt better, like I'd dropped a heavy weight offa me. . . . Hey, now, don't get me wrong. A brave man, the *paisano*, like there ain't very many. But don't forget, this was a dead cinch for me, and to make the cheese more binding, Magdaleno Pérez never misses his first shot."

"So, my friends, by now, you can gather that I'm a good-hearted man," Magdaleno goes on to say as he lays his hand on his breast like a child Jesus. "I was born for a good deed, cause feelin's is feelin's and, take my word, a person has to have self-respect.

"That's what I was sayin to my old *compañero* as we were killin bottle number two at the cantina in San Rafael. We'd been hittin it hard, the Central American way. Nothin like the juice of the cane, is there, to turn tongues loose so's when a pair of old buddies gets together they can cuss one another out a good coupla times, sayin the juiciest goddamn beautiful things comin straight from the heart. Ain't it so? Well, it's also true the bugger don't live can sop up that much rum without blearin over a little. I was good and crocked, I can tell you. And Graciliano maybe a smitch less, just about.

"'Look at that sour puss on the man,' I said, starin square at him, 'when the friend here oughta be happy cause today was his lucky day.' The things you'll come out with when the rum gets to you!

"'And he don't even know why. How could he know? Goddamn, but friendship sure is somethin wonderful. Ain't that so, Graciliano? For friendship there's nothin I wouldn't do. Or, I oughta say,' (and I give out a laugh) 'there's somethin I wouldn't do.'

"Graciliano wouldn't let on a yes or a no. Every once in a while, he looked at me in a sorta funny way, as if he knew what I was thinkin. But I'm not sure, cause his thoughts were comin out kinda glassy, his eyes drowned in the rum.

"'I know who you were waitin for, man . . . I know. Not for a friend, I'll bet, was it?' And I repeated it like a jackass and with a certain intention. *Caramba!* The way a drunk thinks with two thoughts—one up above that goes straight and another underneath that curveballs him.

"But the both of us had the goddamn *conacaste* tree on the brain, all right, all through this. The truth is I kept talkin about the business all the time but without spillin the whole bit, and him, hardly speakin' a word, said over and over, without sayin it, that he couldn't get the blasted appointment out of his head and that he'd took off before the person he was supposed to meet could get there.

"And in the middle of all this he waves for the check.

"'Hey, no way you're gonna pay this!' I broke in on him. But by then, bein as I was hurt in my pride, I followed up sayin to him, 'Well, gettin right down to it, maybe you oughta. The kinda day you had calls for it. Get me? No, you don't get me.'

"What can I tell you? My head like it didn't know front from back and just waitin for a chance to play me dirty, the son of a gun. And when he began makin moves to stand up and get goin, I lit into him again.

"'But why're you leavin? Where do you have to go, anyway? What's the big rush . . . you think that person showed for the appointment? Ha, ha! I tell you no. I know he won't be there. Listen, Ciliano, betcha there ain't no such person. Okay, then tell me who it is. Don't be keepin a friend in the dark. You see, don't you see? You don't even know. He don't exist. Go ahead, then, go on home, take a look at the calendar, and light a candle to today's saint.' Me, pluggin away again.

"'Thanks.' He stood up and started walkin. 'But, now, I really got to get goin.'

"I knew he couldn't get that damn *conacaste* out of his mind and that was where he was off to. Graciliano was a man of his word, I want you to know.

"I yelled to the bartender, 'Quick, settle up and hand me my change. I have to head off that friend and help him home.'

"When I got on my feet, I noticed my legs was wantin to go off on their own. Naturally. We'd been drinkin like men. But, I'd done a good deed and felt proud of myself. What a kick Graciliano would've had out of it if he'd known what a good deed I done him! But there's some people want it all laid out for them.

"'Where you off to?' I said when I caught up with him. 'I'll walk you home.'

"He turned around, not in a nice way, it seemed to me. And he said, 'Listen here, I'm who decides what I do and what I don't do. That's enough, now. You're beginnin to give me a pain in the ass.'

"Aha! So, I was beginnin to give him a pain in the ass. But even then, I couldn't let him go back to the damn tree, on account of somethin told me it wouldn't turn out good for anybody. That was why I kept pluggin away at him not to go, that he should take my word that it would be better for him not to, that he couldn't understand why.

"I was doin' it from the heart, so help me.

"'Listen to me, listen to me,' I repeated to him so many times I get mad even when I think of it. And him, walkin and walkin, until finally he lets me have it.

"'Goddamn it to hell! Now, you're gripin me in the gut for real.' See, that wasn't very nice of Graciliano.

"After all this, we were nearly back at the *conacaste*.

"'You don't know.' I said, grabbin him by the arm. 'Go on back.'

"'*You* don't know, you don't know! You're slob drunk, you jerk! Let up with this crap of yours once and for all.'

"Damn it, he hadn't ought to have done it. . . . He stops short all of a sudden and pushes me one helluva shove. 'I told you to leave me alone, Leno. I know what I have to do!'

"I think that's what he was sayin as I fell over and he turned his back on me and kept goin. When I hit that ground, it hurt, but I mean hurt right to the soul. Ah, no, brother, that's not the way! He asked for it. In my fog, I didn't even know when I pulled my gun and put two slugs into him then and there.

"The man was flat on his face, gaspin his last, as I picked myself up off the ground, and I said, 'He wouldn't listen to me.'"

"The courts? Are you guys kiddin'? The Wheel took care of fixin the ticket. The man that's got it can buy it. If he can buy it, he's got it. Especially when it's to his own benefit. All the witnesses you'd want—" and the little man holds up his two hands, making the sign of the cross with his thumbs and index fingers, "self-defense."

And he opens his arms wide, absolving himself of all blame, as he turns to us again, blinking his eyes with the same expression of ineffable innocence he wore when he'd just returned from Chiquimula.

Translated by Asa Zatz

Authors' Biographies

CLARIBEL ALEGRÍA.   Born in Estelí, Nicaragua, in 1924, she grew up in El Salvador. An outspoken, passionate advocate of the liberation struggle in Central America, she has published (together with her husband, the North American writer Darwin J. Flakoll) several testimonial works on repression in El Salvador and its victims. Alegría has published 14 volumes of poetry and four of short fiction and novellas. Some of her work that has been published in English translation includes: *Flowers from the Volcano*, a collection of poetry translated by Carolyn Forché (Pittsburgh University Press, 1982); *Luisa in Realityland*, translated by Darwin J. Flakoll (Curbstone Press, 1987), and *They Won't Take Me Alive*, a testimonial work of a Salvadoran woman who fought and was killed as a guerrilla (Women Press, 1987). She frequently lectures at universities in the United States. Alegría and her husband live in both Nicaragua and in Marbella, Spain.

MANLIO ARGUETA.   Born in San Miguel, El Salvador, in 1935, he belongs to the generation of writers and poets (Alfonso Quijada Urías, Roque Dalton, Otto René Castillo, among others) who formed a literary circle at the National University in 1956, and who worked in opposition to the military dictatorship that ruled El Salvador. The group's political activities led to persecution, imprisonment, death, and exile. In the mid-1960s, their work began to be known outside of El Salvador, bringing international attention to the plight of the Salvadoran people. Argueta considers himself first and foremost a poet. He has published three volumes of poetry and won, among other awards, the Rubén Darío Poetry Prize, in 1968. He has also published four novels: *El valle de las hamacas* (1970); *Caperucita en la zona roja* (1977), which won the Casa de las Americas prize for Best Novel, 1977; *Un día en la vida* (1980), which won the National Prize given by Catholic University, El Salvador, in 1980 and which was translated into English as *One Day of Life* (Aventura, 1985); and *Cuzcatlán donde bate la mar del sur* (1986), which was also translated into English, as *Cuzcatlán, Where the Southern Sea Beats*, (Aventura, 1987). He lives in Costa Rica, where he is the founder and director of the Salvadoran-Costa Rican Institute and works actively in cultural and political matters concerning Central American countries.

ARTURO ARIAS. Born in Guatemala City, Guatemala, in 1950, he gives as his specialization "sociology of Latin American literature, Indian matters, and the problem of ethnicity in Guatemala." In addition to his collection of stories, *En la ciudad y en las montañas* (1975), and two novels, *Despues de las bombas* (1979) and *Itzam Na* (1981), he coauthored the script of the highly acclaimed film *El Norte*. He is librettist for a forthcoming opera about the Maya-Quiche, "Los Caminos de Paxil," with composer Richard Cameron-Wolfe. His awards include the Casa de las Americas awards for Best Essay, 1979, and Best Novel, 1981 (for *Itzam Na*). Arias has been elected president of the newly organized Congress of Central American writers, which convened in Guatemala in July of 1988.

HORACIO CASTELLANOS MOYA. Born in Tegucigalpa, Honduras, in 1957. He represents what is known as the Central American diaspora. He was born of a Honduran mother and Salvadoran father, and when he was four, his family moved to El Salvador, where he stayed until 1978. He left El Salvador, moving first to Canada and later to Costa Rica. Castellanos Moya writes poetry and fiction. In his two collections of short stories, *¿Qué signo es usted niña Berta?* 1981) and *Perfil de prófugo* (1987), he portrays the lives of politically active young people, either in exile or in their countries, using a matter-of-fact, everyday language that adds a poignant element to the stories. Since 1981, he has lived in Mexico, working as a journalist, and is presently the editor of the magazine, *Voices of Mexico.*

ROBERTO CASTILLO. Born in Tegucigalpa, Honduras, in 1950. Castillo teaches philosophy at the Universidad Nacional Autónoma de Honduras. He has published two collections of short stories, *Subida al cielo y otros cuentos* (1980) and *Figuras de agradable demencia* (1985), and a short novel, *El cometa* (1981). His short story, "La laguna," won Mexico's Plural-Excelsior prize in 1984.

LYZANDRO CHÁVEZ ALFARO. Born in Bluefields, Nicaragua, in 1929. A novelist, short-story writer, essayist and poet, he belongs to the generation of writers who started a "new narrative" in Central America. In his work he deals with his country's realities in a universal context and interprets its own history and culture. Chávez Alfaro's first novel *Trágame tierra* (1969), is considered the first expression of this concern in the new Central American narrative. The novel won the prestigious Seix Barral prize in Barcelona in 1966. He has published two volumes of short stories—*Los monos de San Telmo* (1963), which won the Casa de las Americas prize for 1963, and *Trece veces nunca* (1985)—numerous essays on literary, cultural and political subjects, and two books of poems. At present, he serves as the Ambassador of Nicaragua in Hungary.

FABIAN DOBLES. Born in San Antonio de Belen, Costa Rica, in 1918. Short story writer, poet and novelist, Dobles is the senior writer in this collection, and a major figure of Costa Rican letters, having published more than 20 books to date. His work is characterized by themes deeply rooted in his country's rural life and careful use of vernacular language. He published his first novel, *Ese que llaman pueblo*, in 1942, and his most recent volume of short stories, *La pesadilla y otros cuentos*, in 1985. He received Costa Rica's National Prize for Literature in 1968. His work has been translated into German and Russian.

Jo ANNE ENGELBERT. Born in Cincinnati, Ohio, in 1933 and raised in Kentucky. She has published *Macedonio Fernández and the Spanish American New Novel* (New York University Press, 1978) and *Macedonio* (Latitudes Press, 1984), an anthology of the writings of Macedonio Fernández in English translation. She has also translated stories, essays, and poems by several Latin American writers, including Julio Cortázar, Isabel Allende, and Roberto Sosa. Engelbert has visited Central America frequently in recent years under a Fulbright research grant and is currently working on a bilingual anthology of Central American poetry. She teaches Latin American literature at Montclair State College in Montclair, New Jersey.

JULIO ESCOTO. Born in San Pedro Sula, Honduras, in 1944. Author of novels, short stories and children's books, as well as numerous literary essays and articles. Escoto is the founding director of the Centro Editorial in Tegucigalpa. His latest book is the novel, *Bajo el almendro, junto al volcán* (1988). He has received Honduras' National Prize for Literature (1967) and Spain's Gabriel Miró Literary Prize (1983), the latter for his short story "April in the Forenoon," from his collection, *La balada del herido pájaro* (1985).

JACINTA ESCUDOS. Born in San Salvador, El Salvador, in 1961. The youngest writer in this collection, she left her country at age 19, went to West Berlin, where she stayed for a year, and then returned to Central America. Escudos' work is still scarcely published: *Letter from El Salvador*, a book of poems, was published in London; her first novel, *Apuntes de una historia de amor que no fue*, was recently published in El Salvador. An excerpt of this work appeared in English translation in *Bomb* (Spring/Summer, 1985); her short stories have been published only in literary magazines and supplements in Central America. She lives in Nicaragua, working for a nongovernmental organization that finances health projects, and making documentary films.

AUGUSTO MONTERROSO. Born in Guatemala City, Guatemala, in 1921. By his own admission, a shy and undistinguished student, he left school at age 15 and went to work in a butcher shop. There he made his first serious acquaintance with literature, as his boss encouraged his reading of Shakespeare, Juvenal, Lord Chesterton, Victor Hugo, Madame Sévigné, and Thomas Mann. This reading led to his first writing, but it was not until he moved to Mexico in 1944, that he received any recognition. Monterroso has published more than 14 volumes of satirical short fiction and fables; he is considered a master of the genre throughout Latin America. Only one of Monterroso's books has been translated into English, *The Black Sheep and Other Fables* (Doubleday, 1971, now out-of-print), but he is frequently published in literary magazines and collections. Carlos Fuentes describes Monterroso's work this way: "Imagine Borges' fantastic bestiary having tea with Alice. Imagine Dean Swift and James Thurber trading notes. Imagine a frog from Calaveras County who had actually read Mark Twain. Meet Augusto Monterroso."

MARIO ROBERTO MORALES. Born in Guatemala City, Guatemala, in 1947. He has also lived in Costa Rica, Nicaragua, and Italy. A writer of novels, short stories, poetry, and essays (all published in Guatemala and Costa Rica), he won the Costa Rican 1985 Educa Literary Prize for his novel, *El esplendor de la pirámide*. Morales' novel *Los demonios salvajes* (1977) won the "15 of September" prize in Guatemala, but his work has received limited circulation. A book of essays, a novel, and the English translation of *El esplendor de la pirámide* are still in manuscript. He holds degrees in philosophy, sociology, and Italian art, and presently lives in San José, Costa Rica, where he works as a researcher at the Confederation of Central American Universities.

CARMEN NARANJO. Born in Cartago, Costa Rica, in 1931. She has been an outstanding figure in Costa Rican cultural and political life. Her extensive oeuvre includes six novels, the most recent of which, *Sobrepunto*, was published in 1985; three volumes of published short stories, *Ondina, Hoy es un largo día*, and *Nunca hubo alguna vez*; and one—*Otro rumbo para la rumba*—still in manuscript, from which her story "And We Sold the Rain," presented here, was taken; several volumes of poetry; plays; and essays. She has received Costa Rica's National Prize for Literature twice, and the Magon Prize, the highest honor conferred by the government to an individual, was given to her in recognition of her work on behalf of culture. She has served as Secretary of Culture in Costa Rica, and heads the Editorial Universitaria Centroamericana, the most important publishing organization in Central America.

MARIO PAYERAS. Born in Guatemala in 1950. Active in the guerrilla movement (Poor People's Guerrilla Army) in his country, he wrote a testimonial work, *Los días de la selva* (Casa de las Americas, 1981), recounting his years as a guerrilla spent in the jungle. Subsequent editions of this book have been published in Guatemala (a clandestine edition from the PPGA), in Mexico, Nicaragua, Costa Rica, and Spain. It has been translated and published in West Germany, India, and the United States (*Days of the Jungle*, Monthly Review Press, 1983). Payeras has also written book-length essays on ecology, short stories, poetry, and children's literature, some of which is still unpublished. His study of ecology in his country, *La latitud de la flor y el granizo*, will be published this year in Mexico by Editorial Joan Boldó y Climent.

BERTALICIA PERALTA. Born in Panama in 1939. She published her first book of poems, *Canto de esperanza filial*, in 1962. Thirteen more volumes followed, and they received literary prizes in Panama and Peru. Peralta's short story collection, *Barcarola y otras fantasías incorregibles* was awarded the Premio Universidad from the University of Panama (1973), and the story "Guayacán de Marzo" ("A March Guayacan") was awarded the Premio Literario from the National Institute of Culture. She has also published children's literature, and is a columnist for some of the most important papers in Panama. She is the Director of Information and Public Relations at the University of Panama.

ALFONSO QUIJADA URÍAS. Born in Quezaltepeque, El Salvador, in 1940. He belongs to the generation of Salvadoran poets who, during the 1960s, joined the peasants in their daily demonstrations against the military dictatorship and shared their poems, "The same way we shared bread and tortillas." He remained in El Salvador until 1978 when he moved to Nicaragua and subsequently to Mexico, where he worked as a journalist. His volumes of poetry and short stories have all been published in El Salvador, and in special editions in Havana, Cuba. His work has appeared in anthologies, including City Lights Books' *Volcan*, edited by Lawrence Ferlinghetti (1984), and *Anthologie de la Nouvelle Hispano Americaine* (Paris: Pierre Belfond, 1983). His most recent volume of short stories, *Para mirarte mejor* (1987) was published in Honduras. Quijada Urías' stories are grounded in everyday events from which he extracts the magic instant, the satirical and humorous elements of the human condition. Since 1987, he has lived in Vancouver, Canada, writing a novel.

SERGIO RAMÍREZ. Born in Masatepe, Nicaragua, in 1942. He received his law degree in 1954, lived in Costa Rica and Europe until 1979, and then returned to Nicaragua. He has published three collections of short stories: *Cuentos* (1963), *Nuevos cuentos* (1969), and *Charles Atlas también muere* (*Stories*, Readers International, 1986). His novel, *¿Te dió miedo la sangre?* (1982) has also been translated (*To Bury Our Fathers*, Readers International, 1985). A new novel, *Castigo divino*, was recently published in Barcelona. In his short stories, Ramírez explores the contradictions of Latin American culture, the constant presence of North American influence and the cruel realities of senseless, brutal repression. He has also published essays on Latin American culture and politics. The leading prose writer from Nicaragua, he is now its Vice President.

RODRIGO REY ROSA. Born in Guatemala City, Guatemala, in 1958. While only one collection of his work is published in Spanish, *El cuchillo del mendigo* (Guatemala, 1986), Rey Rosa's work has been published in English in two collections: *The Path Doubles Back* (Red Ozier Press, 1982) and *The Beggar's Knife* (City Lights, 1985). His short stories have appeared in *Frank Magazine* (Paris), *City Lights Review*, and *Threepenny Review*. Rey Rosa has been living in Tangier, Morocco, since 1980, where he met author Paul Bowles. His stories, based in myths and beliefs indigenous to Central America and North Africa, caught the attention of Bowles, who began to translate them into English.

PEDRO RIVERA. Born in Panama City, Panama, in 1939. He has published six volumes of poetry and one collection of short stories. *Los pájaros regresan de la niebla* (1969) received the Ricardo Miró Prize for poetry, as did his short-story collection, *Peccata minuta* (Panama, 1970). Rivera is actively involved with film, and has made more than 30 documentaries, some of which have been honored at international competitions. He is the director of the Experimental Film Group at the University of Panama, editor of the film magazine, *Cine Formato 16*, and of the supplementary, *Temas de Nuestra América*. Together with Panamanian author Dimas Lidio Pitty, he recently published a new collection of short stories in *Recuentos* (Colección Labrapalabra, 1988).

SAMUEL ROVINSKI. Born in San José, Costa Rica, in 1932. With a degree in civil engineering, he is a prolific writer of fiction, drama, and essays. He has published more than 18 books and has three in manuscript. Rovinski has also written film scripts, one of which (*La guerra de los filibusteros*) won a bronze medal in the International Film Festival in New York (1982). In his fiction he chronicles the human miseries of urban life that provoke "mute" violence. He has also written about the Jews in Central America in his collection of short stories *Cuentos judíos de mi tierra* (1982). He has been awarded Costa Rica's National Prize in Theater (1975) for his play "Un modelo para Rosaura" and the National Prize for Best Novel (1976) for *Ceremonia de casta*.

LEONEL RUGAMA. Born in Estelí, Nicaragua, March 27, 1949. He was killed in Managua, January 15, 1970, at age 20, when he was preparing to join the guerrillas in the mountains. He is remembered as an intensely serious, but witty, man who loved poetry and had strong convictions about the revolutionary process. He met Omar Cabezas (author of *Fire in the Mountain*, 1986) while in high school, and both went along the same path of struggle for liberation. Cabezas remembers Rugama with these words:

> I was influenced by Leonel, but not just in a literary way; in my life. I was influenced . . . by [his] way of thinking, of making things happen. . . . I began to write, but I didn't know how to. I never really read literature. . . . It has to do with Leonel. Because we had fun with a whole world of things, and years later I would be thinking how he would have liked this . . . and I thought all this shit is going to be lost; and the epic of the mountains, and our struggle. . . . So I began to write: for Leonel. This whole thing has something to do with him.

During his short life, Rugama wrote poetry and prose, which was collected in one volume, published in Nicaragua in 1978, and translated into English (*The Earth Is a Satellite of the Moon*, Curbstone Press, 1985). His poetry is a reflection of his political thought and of his vision of social injustice and oppression. At age 19, Rugama wrote a manifesto, "The Student and the Revolution," that influenced many young Nicaraguans.

ROSARIO SANTOS.   Born in La Paz, Bolivia, in 1942. She has been the managing editor of the literary journal *Review, Latin American Art and Literature* and the director of the literature program of the Center for Inter-American Relations. She has been living and working in New York since 1960, involved in literary and cultural activities related to Latin America. She works for the Institute of International Education, in charge of Fulbright Programs for Latin America.

Translators' Biographies

ZÖE ANGLESEY is a poet. She has frequently translated Central American authors for literary magazines, collections, and anthologies. She has edited the anthologies, *Ixok Amar-go: Central American Women's Poetry for Peace*, and *Voices of New Women*.

PAUL BOWLES is a novelist, short-story writer, and composer. He has translated extensively works from French, Spanish, and Maugrabin. He has resided in Tangier, Morocco, for the past 40 years.

NICK CAISTOR is a London-based journalist who works as Latin American researcher for *Index of Censorship* magazine. He has translated the work of, among others, Claribel Alegría and Julio Cortázar. He translated Sergio Ramaírez' first novel to appear in English, *To Bury Our Fathers*.

JO ANNE ENGELBERT. See Authors' Biographies.

DARWIN J. FLAKOLL is a journalist. In collaboration with his wife, Claribel Alegría, he has published testimonial works dealing with the struggle in El Salvador and Nicaragua, and has translated into Spanish the work of Robert Graves and an anthology of North American poetry. He has also translated into English Claribel Alegría's *Luisa in Realityland*.

EDITH GROSSMAN is a critic and translator of contemporary Latin American literature. The author of *The Anti-Poetry of Nicanor Parra* and of numerous articles and reviews, she is also the translator of major contemporary Hispanic writers' works—most recently of Gabriel García Márquez's *Love in the Time of Cholera*. She teaches at Dominican College in Orangeburg, New York, and resides in New York City.

211

CLARK HANSEN has an M.A. in comparative literature from New York University. Other published translations of his include Ariel Dorfman's *The Empire's Old Clothes*. He lives in southern California with his wife and daughter.

ANN KOSHEL is a poet from New York City where she teaches English for various Higher Educational Opportunities programs.

GREGORY RABASSA has translated over 30 books of Latin American literature over the past two decades, among them major works by Gabriel García Márquez, Mario Vargas Llosa, Julio Cortázar and Jorge Amado. His work has merited an array of awards, including the PEN Translation Prize and recently, the Wheatland Foundation Award for his "notable contribution to international literary exchange."

RICHARD SCHAAF has translated the works of Salvadoran poet Roque Dalton, including his poetry, the testimonial novel *Miguel Marmol*, and the book of essays *A Red Book for Lenin*. He translated two books of essays by César Vallejo, and co-translated Leonel Rugama's *The Earth Is a Satellite of the Moon*.

CYNTHIA VENTURA is a freelance interpreter and translator. Her translations of Luisa Valenzuela, Rosario Ferré, and Carmen Lugo Fillipi, have been published in *Translation*, *The Review of Contemporary Fiction*, and *Review, Latin American Literature and Arts*.

GEORGE YÚDICE teaches Latin American literature at Hunter College in New York City. He has translated various Central American authors, including Claribel Alegría.

ASA ZATZ has translated plays by Austrian playright Ferdinand Bruchner and the writings of anthropologist Oscar Lewis, including Lewis' *The Children of Sanchez*. At present he translates the work of selected authors, including Gabriel García Márquez (*Clandestine in Chile*), Alejo Carpentier (*Concierto Barroco*), and Tomás Eloy Martínez (*The Perón Novel*).

Acknowledgments

"Look at Lislique, See How Pretty It Is" ("Mira Lislique, qué bonito . . .") by Jacinta Escudos (El Salvador). Originally published in the literary supplement of El Día, San Salvador (1982). Published here in English for the first time by permission of the author. Translation copyright © 1988 by George Yúdice.

"The Proof" ("La prueba") by Rodrigo Rey Rosa (Guatemala). First published in English in City Lights Review (1987). Published here by permission of the author. Translation copyright © 1987 by Paul Bowles.

"Anita the Insect Catcher" (Anita, la cazadora de insectos") by Roberto Castillo (Honduras). Originally published in his collection of short stories, Subida al cielo y otros cuentos (1980). Published here in English for the first time by permission of the author. Translation copyright © 1988 by Cynthia Ventura.

"Confinement" ("Encierro") by Horacio Castellanos Moya (El Salvador). Originally published in his collection of short stories, Perfil de prófugo (1987). Published here in English for the first time by permission of the author. Translation copyright © 1988 by George Yúdice.

"I Am René Espronceda de la Barca" ("Yo soy René Espronceda de la Barca") by Leonel Rugama (Nicaragua). First published in English in The Earth is a Satellite of the Moon (Willimantic, CT: Curbstone Press, 1985). Reprinted here by permission of Curbstone Press. Translation copyright © 1985 by Richard Schaaf, Sara Miles and Nancy Weisberg.

"For These Things My Name Is René" (excerpt from the novel Los demonios salvajes, 1977) by Mario Roberto Morales (Guatemala). Published here in English for the first time by permission of the author. Translation copyright © 1988 by Asa Zatz.

"April in the Forenoon" ("Abril antes del mediodía") by Julio Escoto (Honduras). Originally published in his collection of short stories, La balada del herido pájaro (1985). Published here in English for the first time